PRINCIPAL
LEADERSHIP

To America

The Lord bless you and keep you.
The Lord make His face to shine upon you and be gracious to you.
The Lord lift up His countenance upon you
and give you peace.

Numbers 6:24–26

God bless America,
All Americans,
The victims' families of the September 11, 2001, terrorist attack,
My wonderful family, friends, and students,
And our schools.

PRINCIPAL LEADERSHIP

APPLYING THE NEW EDUCATIONAL LEADERSHIP
CONSTITUENT COUNCIL (ELCC) STANDARDS

FOREWORD BY
JOHN R. HOYLE

ELAINE L. WILMORE

CORWIN PRESS, INC.
A Sage Publications Company
Thousand Oaks, California

For information:

Corwin Press, Inc.
A Sage Publications Company
2455 Teller Road
Thousand Oaks, California 91320
E-mail: order@corwinpress.com

Sage Publications Ltd.
6 Bonhill Street
London EC2A 4PU
United Kingdom

Sage Publications India Pvt. Ltd.
M-32 Market
Greater Kailash I
New Delhi 110 048 India

Printed in the United States of America

Library of Congress Cataloging-in-Publication Data

Wilmore, Elaine L.
  Principal leadership: Applying the new Educational Leadership
Constituent Council (ELCC) standards / Elaine L. Wilmore.
      p. cm.
Includes bibliographical references and index.
  ISBN 0-7619-4554-7
  ISBN 0-7619-4555-5 (pbk.)
1. School principals—In-service training—Standards—United States.
2. Interns (Education)—United States. I. Title.
  LB2831.92 .W55 2002
  371.2´012´07155—dc21

                                                    2002001600

This book is printed on acid-free paper.

    03 04 05 10 9 8 7 6 5 4 3 2

Acquisitions Editor:	Robb Clouse
Editorial Assistant:	Erin Buchanan
Copy Editor:	Elizabeth Budd
Production Editor:	Denise Santoyo
Typesetter:	Siva Math Setters, Chennai, India
Indexer:	Kathy Paparchontis
Cover Designer:	Michael Dubowe
Production Artist:	Sandra Ng

Contents

Foreword

Elaine Wilmore has made a major contribution to the preparation of school principals with this book. Since the development of the 1983 American Association of School Administrators (AASA) Guidelines for the Preparation of School Administrators, several organizations have extended and modified the seven competencies into standards for the preparation and professional development of school leaders. Fenwick English and Betty Steffy collaborated with me in *Skills for Successful 21st Century School Leaders* (1998) to synthesize the key standards, skills, dispositions, input and outcome measures, and instructional strategies included in standards by the AASA, Educational Leadership Constituent Council (ELCC), National Council for the Accreditation of Teacher Education (NCATE), National Policy Board for Educational Administration (NPBEA), and the Interstate School Leaders Licensure (ISLLC). In 2001, the ELCC, composed of selected individuals representing AASA, AACTE, ASCD, CCSSO, NAESP, NASSP, NCPEA, and UCEA, revised standards for Advanced Programs in Educational Leadership and presented them to the Specialty Areas Study Board (SASB) of NCATE. These new ELCC standards for principals, superintendents, and other central office administrators were drawn from ISLLC, AASA, and NCATE standards for the position of superintendent and other central office administrators. They represent the latest collaboration of professional associations to establish the vital elements to judge the quality of preparation programs for school leaders.

Now Elaine Wilmore has taken a bold step in writing this important book on principal leadership by focusing on the ELCC standards for the preparation of campus-level principals. Dr. Wilmore brings to her scholarship successful experience from public-school classrooms and principalships, from the boardroom, and from the university where she has been a leader in the creation of one of the nation's most respected field-based programs for school principals. In this definitive work, Dr. Wilmore presents multiple examples of problem-based teaching and field-based learning to prepare informed, skilled, and caring principals for the elementary, middle, and high schools of America. Elaine Wilmore's content mastery blends scholarship with practice to guide program planners in gaining ELCC approval and NCATE accreditation and to prepare the best and the brightest for the demanding role of principal.

Dr. Wilmore has earned the respect of practitioners, state and national association executives, and her colleagues in higher education. She is President Elect of the National Council of Professors of Educational Administration and has the reputation of a dynamic and positive spokesperson in our discipline. This book is a must for all program directors striving for excellence in principal preparation and for those interested in earning NCATE accreditation.

John R. Hoyle

Preface

Principal Leadership: Applying the New Educational Leadership
Constituent Council (ELCC) Standards was written to address
the new standards for the preparation and development of school
principals created jointly by the National Council for the Accreditation of Teacher Education (NCATE) and the Interstate School
Leaders Licensure Consortium (ISLLC). These standards, known as
the Educational Leadership Constituent Council standards, are of
critical importance in creating, nurturing, and sustaining a culture
and climate that values the soul of the school within its political,
social, economic, legal, and cultural context. Although a myriad of
books exist on school leadership, climate, and change, this book
is the first to connect the new standards to the philosophy and implementation of the principal as steward of the school's vision. *Principal Leadership* addresses these connections from the perspective
of the school as essential to the essence and success of a school
learning community.

   This book is unique and timely in format. At long last the separate
administrative standards and guidelines of the NCATE and the ISLLC
have merged into one set of collaboratively developed and agreed-
upon standards for the development of future school leaders and for
the professional growth of existing ones. No book has addressed these
merged standards, making *Principal Leadership* both distinctive and
opportune. It is written within a context of tying the new standards to
practical yet research-based applications for principals and others
interested in school leadership. Based on eminent leadership and

management theory and research, *Principal Leadership* is written in an informative manner, yet it is also practical, readable, interesting, insightful, and inspiring. Future administrators may use it as a text for university coursework in school leadership. Current administrators can use it for individual or group reflective professional development.

Principal Leadership addresses both a global, proactive philosophy of school leadership as provided in the ELCC standards and specific treatment of the components within each standard. This is done through discussion, case studies, reflective questions and activities, and "The Ultimate Application" for individual or groups engaged in professional development opportunities. It is appropriate for preservice and current principals, assistant principals, deans of instruction, instructional supervisors, educational and other professional associations, and anyone interested in the development and nurturance of the school community. The text is divided into three sections. The first section is introductory in nature. The second focuses on each of the seven ELCC standards. The final section pulls all the components together and draws conclusions. A selection of additional readings for each standard is provided for supplementary conceptual purposes.

Principal Leadership is a must-read for those preparing for school leadership positions as well as for practitioners seeking to stretch beyond their comfort zones in our changing world. It provides a framework of the standards and tools necessary to facilitate school leaders' work with students, teachers, families, and communities in a collaborative partnership. If you are ready to make this commitment—knowing it will require hard work, focus, and persistence—read on. This is the book for you!

ACKNOWLEDGMENTS

During the final days of writing this book, terrorists attacked the United States, our freedom, and our way of life. All of America was shocked by this blatant and violent attempt to harm us. But the attack spawned renewed vision and purpose as all Americans came together in a shared sense of purpose and patriotism. Other societal issues have become blurred as we speak with a single, united voice.

As educators we, too, must develop this sense of urgency and passion as we speak with one voice for the needs of children and their families. This book provides a framework of the newly developed Educational Leadership Constituent Council standards for the preparation and development of school leaders. It provides a tool to use our unified voice to meet specific standards and goals. This is something we have needed for a long time.

Many important people in my life have been instrumental in facilitating both the development of the standards and the writing of this book. Although I cannot possibly acknowledge them all, there are some individuals whom I must recognize. As always, my family has been wonderful, working to spare me from as many interruptions as possible so I could focus and write. Thank you, Greg, Mother, Brandon, Brittani, and Brooke. In particular I thank Brittani for her conscientious editing, knowing she offered her time when she would rather have been doing almost anything else. Without her, I could not possibly have completed this work on time. Thank you, sweetie! You are our wonderful gift.

Thank you to Honor Fede, Folio Coordinator for the Educational Leadership Constituent Council, for her assistance in preparing this manuscript. In addition to being one of the nicest people in the world, Honor is always helpful to the developers of programs undergoing review as well as to individuals seeking information. Thank you, Honor, for being the committed professional that you are, for being so knowledgeable, and for being so kind to everyone.

Thank you to the University of Texas at Arlington and particularly to my dean, Dr. Jeanne M. Gerlach, for supporting and encouraging me in every facet of my writing. Thank you for encouraging me always to go beyond any limits in pursuing excellence.

Thank you to Dr. John R. Hoyle, my mentor and friend, for believing and expecting the best in me and then showing how proud of me he is. John, you will never know how much it means to my life to make you proud.

I don't know what I would have done or could ever do without my true and sincere friend, Dr. Linda Norman Townzen. Thank you,

Linda, for always looking out for me, caring about me, being my champion, and constantly urging me to get some sleep. You are a dream of a friend.

Thank you also to all my wonderful friends who stand beside me and encourage me in my quiet revolution to "change the world, one school at a time." Thank you particularly to Dr. Bob and Becky Shaw for their love and continuous generosity in providing me a safe, quiet mountain retreat to write, reflect, and refocus on who I am, why I am here, and what is truly important in my life. There is no way I can ever put into words what your generosity and support means to me. You have done this for many years. I hope from the bottom of my heart that you never stop. You are blessings in the lives of so many, especially us. Thank you both so much.

Last, to America, who could say it better than the psalmist:

Restore us, Oh God.

Psalm 80:3

All my love,

Elaine

About the Author

Elaine Litchfield Wilmore, Ph.D., is Special Assistant to the Dean for NCATE Accreditation and an Associate Professor of Educational Leadership and Policy Studies at the University of Texas at Arlington, She is also President of Elaine L. Wilmore Leadership Initiatives. She is the founding Director of School Administration Programs at the University of Texas at Arlington, Educational Leadership UTA, and the Scholars of Practice innovative programs for which she has received external grants. She has served as Chair of Educational Administration and Director of University Program Development, and is currently Chair of the UTA School of Education Faculty Governance Committee. She is President-Elect of the National Council of Professors of Educational Administration where she also serves on the Executive Board. In addition, Wilmore is active on many other local, state, and national boards, including the Texas Principals Leadership Initiative and her local school board. She has served as President of the Texas Professors of Educational Administration and was a member of the original cadre of program/ folio reviewers for the Educational Leadership Constituent Council for NCATE. Wilmore is known in Texas as the "ExCET Queen" for her statewide success in helping students pass administrative certification examinations.

Wilmore is a former public school teacher, counselor, and elementary and middle school principal. She is in her second term on the Cleburne Independent School District Board of Trustees, serving as Vice President. A frequent national speaker and author, she is known for inspiring others to greatness. In addition to her significant work in the area of administrator development, she enjoys singing in her church choir, reading, writing, and spending time with those she loves. She is married and the mother of three wonderful children, a big boxer dog, and a mutt-cat named Yum.

PART ONE

Introduction

CHAPTER ONE

Our Changing World and Schools

The Need for a Learning Community

It is not news to hear that our world is changing. Unless you are a hermit who has absolutely no contact with the outside world, the change in American culture comes as no surprise. Society is becoming increasingly diverse in race, culture, and language. The hard-and-fast rules that once applied to gender are no more. This is particularly evident in the home and the workplace. The stereotypical two-parent household of a generation ago has steadily eroded. In the past, parents' traditional roles were for the father to go to work to support the family while the mother stayed home, taking care of the children and the household.

In many homes, that image no longer exists. As more mothers work outside the home, latchkey children are quickly becoming the norm. Two-parent households are only a dream for many children. The longitudinal effects of basic family changes like these and their impact on children and schools have yet to be thoroughly studied and communicated. Even if they had been, with the changing mores in the United States today, we have no data-driven conclusions as to what effect, if any, the long-term results would have.

Our schools are microcosms of this changing social order. Things that are happening in urban, suburban, and rural settings obviously manifest themselves in classrooms. Schools no longer, if ever they did,

3

operate independently of the communities in which they exist. The true issue becomes this: How do we as educational leaders address these changes and their effects on the children we serve? This is the focus of the "learning community" or "school community" concept. The days when schools could even think about operating in isolation are long gone. Schools and communities must work together, hand in hand, to meet the staggering academic, physical, and emotional needs of all students. Collaborative development, implementation, nurturance, and stewardship of the school as a "community" are essential to the overall success of students, families, and society.

THE ROLE OF THE PRINCIPAL

The role of the principal has also changed. In past generations, the primary function of the principal evolved from "principal teacher," as a master teacher who also tended to the limited duties required to keep the school organized and operating efficiently, to the principal as the chief executive officer of the campus. The primary emphasis has shifted from one in which the principal truly was a master teacher, a recognized leader in instruction, to one in which the principal is a manager of the school facility. Bureaucracy has grown. Policies, rules, and paperwork have flourished. Societal problems have evolved. The seesaw of responsibility has shifted from curriculum and instruction to management and operations. A transition took place in which the principal became responsible for holding together the walls of the school and ensuring that it runs smoothly. The "principal teacher" thus became the school's organizational manager.

While this was happening, society as a whole continued to evolve. When the United States was primarily agrarian, students left school early to work in the fields. During the Industrial Age, they dropped out of school to fill positions in the lucrative job market. Educators were not particularly worried about these "dropouts." Schools did not spend undue time or effort trying to bring them back to graduate. The casual acceptance of students leaving school early to go to work was symptomatic of the culture of the day.

Times have changed. Particularly with the impact of *A Nation at Risk* (National Commission on Excellence in Education, 1983), the effective schools of research of Ron Edmonds and others, and the accountability movement (Haertel, 1999; Lashway, 2001; McNeil, 2000; Smith, Heinecke, & Noble, 1999; Wellstone, 2000), a renewed interest and focus has been placed on ensuring that every student has access to free and appropriate learning opportunities. The emphasis on high-stakes testing in particular has had an impact on schools attempting to individualize their approaches according to the unique needs of every learner. Focused attempts are made to see that at-risk students can and do pass these tests.

With this increased focus on accountability and student success, another transition has occurred in school leadership. The role of the principal has transitioned again from school manager to the school catalyst for success for all stakeholders. When looking at the campus as a single element rather than the only element within the community, the role of the principal becomes that of school liaison for all community resources including parents and other caregivers, neighbors, businesses, churches, civic clubs, and other community service agencies. The role of the principal becomes the primary voice of the school, the champion of free and appropriate education for all students, and the chief proponent of the value of education in a democratic society. In other words, the principal becomes the main educational facilitator of the learning community.

Expectations

Has the job become one with such high expectations that no one can accomplish them? There are those who think so. Many principals are retiring or leaving the field for a myriad of reasons. Some are tired and battle scarred from leading the crusade for so long. Others have begun to think the gains are not worth the bruises. Still others realize they can make more money elsewhere and choose to do so. There is a documented and growing shortage of people prepared to meet the increased demands and responsibilities that weigh so heavily on the principal's shoulders (Fenwick & Pierce, 2001; Million, 1998;

Potter, 2001; Richardson, 1999; "Study Warns," 1998; U. S. Bureau of Labor Statistics, 2000–2001).

For many educators—thank goodness—all the trials and tribulations that go with being a principal do not outweigh the joys and triumphs of trying to make a difference in the lives of young people every day. Is this a calling? Yes, it is. It requires a personal mission. Are there people occupying these positions who do not feel the calling, yet have the jobs anyway? Disappointingly, yes, there are. Stephen Covey (1990b), Kenneth Blanchard and Spencer Johnson (1982), Valorie Burton (1999), and many others have pointed to the importance of each person reflecting seriously to identify their own mission and then subsequently developing a personal mission statement. Only when we know ourselves and our unique calling can we most prudently plan exactly what we are going to do to achieve it. We are never as effective working outside our individual calling as we could be if we were heeding the intrinsic yearnings of our own hearts.

Is This Book for You?

This book is for many kinds of people. It is for today's principals seeking diligently to find the best ways to benefit the lives of everyone involved in their school communities. It is also for future educational leaders—the countless teachers, coaches, counselors, diagnosticians, paraprofessionals, and others who feel the calling and are either uncertain if the principalship is truly for them or simply do not know how to integrate the idealism of the way schools should be into the reality of the way they actually are. It is also for university faculty seeking to integrate the new joint National Council for the Accreditation of Teacher Education (NCATE)–Interstate School Leaders Licensure Consortium (ISLLC) standards for educational leaders into coursework. This book provides ways to do just that in a practical, easy-to-read manner, using real-life case studies, applications, and reflective open-ended questions that students can relate to and benefit from.

This is a "how-to" book for anyone interested in making a difference in the lives of students, faculty, staff, families, and the entire learning community. It is based on years of research generously provided by such groups as the National Policy Board for Educational Administration, NCATE, ISLLC, Educational Leadership Constituent Council, Council of Chief State School Officers, and virtually all the professional educator associations. For years each group and many states have had their own set of "standards," "proficiencies," or "domains" by which they believe schools should be led. Only now have the professional entities come together, through intense collaboration, dialogue, and discourse, to adopt a common set of standards to facilitate improved school leadership and school leadership preparation.

THE ELCC STANDARDS FOR SCHOOL LEADERS

This new framework is commonly called the Educational Leadership Constituent Council standards, or the ELCC standards. The standards will be used both to strengthen leadership preparation programs and to serve as a cornerstone for the professional development of existing administrators (Council of Chief State School Officers, 1996; McCown, Arnold, Miles, & Hargadine, 2000; Murphy & Shipman, 1998; Murphy, Shipman, & Pearlman, 1997; Murphy, Yff, & Shipman, 2000; Shipman, Topps, & Murphy, 1998; Van Meter & Murphy, 1997). This book is for you or your students if you are committed to making things better; to accepting and addressing high standards based on theory, knowledge, and best practice; and to learning how to make the standards relevant. This is the place to take that first, proactive step toward integrating theory with practice and crossing that huge mountain that exists between idealism and realism. If you are ready to begin that tremendous journey, read on. Invite friends and colleagues to come with you. Together, in critical mass, we will make a difference. Let's begin.

CHAPTER TWO

Standards for the Learning Community

To have a full understanding of the standards, we must know their history. Where did they come from? What are they about? Who developed them? What are they for? What is their purpose and function? In short, why do we need them?

A BRIEF HISTORY: THE STANDARDS STORY

For years, each professional organization and most states have had their own set of proficiencies, domains, standards, or some other term used to describe attributes of principal expectations and job performance. Yet there has not been a unified national set of criteria with far reaching application implications. This left an obvious void as states and organizations sought to move forward and work collaboratively toward commonly developed goals. Although each set had admirable qualities, the effect in the field was an inconsistent moving target of expectations. There was no common set of research-based national standards toward which entities or individuals could work.

The National Policy Board
for Educational Administration

The National Policy Board for Educational Administration (NPBEA) was founded in 1988 by 10 professional organizations with the purpose of improving school leadership (National Policy Board for Educational Administration, 2001). Their bylaws state their purpose as advancing the professional standards of educational administration by collective action (National Policy Board for Educational Administration, 2001). These organizations were the American Association of Colleges for Teacher Education, American Association of School Administrators, Association of School Business Officials, Association for Supervision and Curriculum Development, Council of Chief State School Officers, National Association of Secondary School Principals, (NASSP) National Association of Elementary School Principals (NAESP), National Council of Professors of Educational Administration, National School Boards Association, and University Council for Educational Administration. Under the direction of Executive Secretary Scott Thomson, this work resulted in the definitive *Principals for Our Changing Schools: The Knowledge and Skill Base* (Thomson, 1993). This broad national work is widely used by both preparation programs and current principals seeking professional development. In July of the same year, the NPBEA Board of Directors presented two additional goals:

- To develop common and higher standards for the state licensure of principals
- To develop a common set of guidelines for the National Council for the Accreditation of Teacher Education (NCATE) accreditation of advanced programs in Educational Leadership (National Policy Board for Educational Administration, 2001)

The NPBEA Board of Directors appointed a working group, made up of representatives from all 10 NPBEA organizations, to develop this proposed set of guidelines for NCATE.

Educational Leadership Constituent Council

An NPBEA working group made up of representatives from the Association for Curriculum and Supervision Development, the American Association of School Administrators, the National Association of Elementary School Principals, and the American Association of Secondary School Principals volunteered to pay the costs for administering the completed guidelines for NCATE. This working group became known as the Educational Leadership Constituent Council (ELCC). During the next year, its members worked diligently on the proposed guidelines. These 1995 guidelines used the previous research base of considerable groups. These included various works such as the NPBEA *Principals for Our Changing Schools: The Knowledge and Skill Base* (1993), the *Proposed NCATE Curriculum Guidelines for the Specialty Area of Educational Leadership* published by ASCD (1993), the AASA *Professional Standards for the Superintendency* (1993), the 1988 NAESP *Proficiencies for Principals, K–8* (which were revised in 1993), and the *Framework for the Continual Professional Development of Administrators* (which was published by Region 1 of the Department of Education and the Northeast States in 1993). Various assessment and diagnostic inventories developed by NAESP and NASSP were also used. This draft was sent out for consideration by various university professors and groups before the guidelines were submitted to the National Policy Board and NCATE for review. The subsequent guidelines were used for the appraisal of university-advanced programs in educational administration seeking NCATE accreditation.

Council of Chief State School Officers

The Council of Chief State School Officers (CCSSO) is the national organization of leaders of state departments of education or heads of other departments of elementary and secondary education. Its membership also includes members of the Department of Defense Education Activity, officials from the District of Columbia and other extra-state jurisdictions. CCSSO members seek consensus on major educational issues and are a voice to Congress, federal organizations, professional organizations, and the public (Van Meter & Murphy, 1997).

In 1994, the CCSSO, under the direction of Executive Director Gordon Ambach, who was also a member of the National Policy Board, developed the Interstate School Leaders Licensure Consortium to develop a framework for redefining school leadership through standards for Educational Leadership (Murphy & Shipman, 1998; Murphy, Shipman, & Pearlman, 1997; Shipman, Topps, & Murphy, 1998).

Interstate School Leaders Licensure Consortium

Like the State Education Assessment Center, the Interstate School Leaders Licensure Consortium (ISLLC) is a subset organization of the CCSSO. It was founded in August 1994 with contributions from 24 member states, a large grant from the Pew Charitable Trusts, assistance from the Danforth Foundation, the National Policy Board for Educational Administration, and numerous professional organizations. The purpose of ISLLC is to foster ways for states to work collaboratively to develop and implement assessments, professional development activities, and licensing procedures for school leaders. Its goals are to raise the bar for school leaders and to redefine Educational Leadership (Van Meter & Murphy, 1997).

ISLLC sponsors many professional development activities linked to the standards. These include the School Leaders Licensure Assessment, the School Superintendent's Assessment, and the Portfolio Assessment for School Leaders. In addition, with support from the Pew Foundation, they published *Standards Based Professional Development for School Leaders* (2000) and *Collaborative Professional Development for School Leaders* (2000) to enhance the development of existing administrators.

National Council for the Accreditation of Teacher Education

As part of its continuing quest for timeliness and excellence, NCATE requires all program guidelines be updated and reviewed every 5 years. In addition, NCATE underwent a revision of its own accreditation process in 2000. This reorientation resulted in changes to the way all programs would be assessed. The NCATE focus shifted to a performance-based paradigm to ascertain if graduates are prepared to function in real-world settings (National Policy Board for Educational Administration, 2001).

During this time, the Interstate School Leaders Licensure Consortium had been developed. Also under the indirect guidance of the National Policy Board, ISLLC developed similar standards for educational leaders. It was awkward for universities to deal with two separate sets of criteria. In addition, the working group had a goal of establishing standards for the review of doctoral-level programs in educational administration that lead to the training of practitioners. At this point, the National Policy Board directed the committee working on revising the ELCC guidelines to incorporate the ISLLC standards (National Policy Board for Educational Administration, 2001). The resulting joint set of standards would provide a consistent framework across all entities working together to improve school leadership preparation and professional development. The revised standards were subsequently adopted by NCATE. Although further editing of the standards wording occurred after this book went to press, the philosophy and intent remain the same.

The *ISLLC Standards for School Leaders* (1996) are similar to the ELCC guidelines because of both groups' cooperative relationship with the National Policy Board. The ISLLC standards were adopted in 1996 and are in use throughout the country. The ELCC guidelines have been revised to incorporate both the performance-based direction NCATE is pursuing and the ISLLC standards. This provides for a consistent set of criteria for preparation programs and the professional development of existing school leaders.

THE STANDARDS

To ensure consistency of purpose and to serve as guiding concepts, ISLLC used seven principles in the development of the original standards. They determined all proposed standards should

- Reflect the centrality of student learning
- Acknowledge the changing role of the school leader

- Recognize the collaborative nature of school leadership
- [Upgrade] the quality of the profession
- Inform performance-based systems of assessment and evaluation for school leaders
- Be integrated and coherent
- Be predicated on the concepts of access, opportunity, and empowerment for all members of the school community (Council of Chief State School Officers, 1996, p. 7)

Developers acknowledged that various school leadership roles (i.e., principal, superintendent, curriculum director, etc.) can require different skills; however, there are some tenets of school leadership that are generic to all positions. Originally there were only six standards. The seventh standard regarding the internship was developed and added from the NPBEA Working Group as they revised the ELCC guidelines. In short, the NPBEA Working Group used the ISLLC framework in the initial revision of the original ELCC guidelines. The internship standard is unique to the new ELCC standards. Regardless, each standard focuses "on matters of learning and teaching and the creation of powerful learning environments" (Council of Chief State School Officers, 1996, p. 8). Toward this end, each standard begins with the same important phrase: "A school administrator is an educational leader who promotes the success of all students by . . .".

Having learned the background and development of the new ELCC standards, it is time to see the resulting standards.

A school administrator is an educational leader who promotes the success of all students by . . .

1. Facilitating the development, articulation, implementation, and stewardship of a school or district vision of learning that is shared and supported by the school community

2. Advocating, nurturing, and sustaining a school culture and instructional program conducive to student learning and staff professional growth

3. Ensuring management of the organization, operations, and resources for a safe, efficient, and effective learning environment

4. Collaborating with families and community members, responding to diverse community interests and needs, and mobilizing community resources

5. Acting with integrity, fairness, and in an ethical manner

6. Understanding, responding to, and influencing the larger political, social, economic, legal, and cultural context

7. Substantial, sustained, standards-based experiences in real settings that are planned and guided cooperatively by university and school district personnel for graduate credit

WHY?

It is obvious that a great deal of work and resources have gone into the development of these joint ELCC standards. Some may ask, "Why? What's the big deal? What real relationship do a set of national standards have on practitioners who actually lead schools today or who hope to lead them tomorrow?"

In the classic musical *South Pacific,* Bloody Mary sings a song called "Happy Talk." In it she admonishes her daughter and a young navy officer that they must have a dream. If you do not have a dream, how can you have a dream come true? In like manner, motivational speaker Les Brown encourages others to reach for the moon. Even if you miss it, you will land among the stars. It amounts to the vision of excellence for the school and becomes a matter of high expectations. You reap what you sow. Dream big; get big results. But if you set minimum standards or expectations, that's exactly what you'll get. Either way, you reap what you sow.

Are the standards dreams? Definitely not. However, they do provide us with specific goals of the way our schools could be if we could turn reality into idealism. They provide high goals. If we reach for the moon and don't quite make it, we'll still land among the stars. For many of our schools today, landing in the stars is a big step forward from where they are now.

These joint standards provide all school leaders with a common framework for attaining excellence. Everyone of us, each and every day, should be planning strategies and techniques to help facilitate our schools in becoming the nurturing, sustaining places described in these standards. What if every school and learning community in the United States made a conscious effort to collaboratively develop, implement, and evaluate everything they do such that every campus attained them? Would that not be significant improvement from where we are now?

This is school leadership as it should be. Will striving for this excellence be an easy task? Of course not. Nothing worthwhile is ever easy. The same is true in school leadership. No pain, no gain. Most campuses are making a genuine effort to improve. It's not time to work harder; it's time to work smarter. The ELCC standards provide the framework necessary to build dreams, to reach for the moon, and to create schools that are better, more nurturing, and more successful environments where teachers teach and students learn. Isn't that what education is supposed to be all about?

Now let's begin studying the seven standards.

PART TWO

Application of the Standards

CHAPTER THREE

Creating the Vision of a Collaborative Learning Community

STANDARD 1:

A school administrator is an educational leader who promotes the success of all students by facilitating the development, articulation, implementation, and steward-ship of a school or district vision of learning that is shared and supported by the school community.

As we begin the study of the standards, it is important to look at the common way each of them begins, "A school admini-strators is an educational leader who promotes the success of all students by. . . ." Of course. If we are not here to promote the success of all students, then why are we here? We are not here to promote only the education of those who are easy to teach, who speak English fluently, who fit school in between before-school athletics and after-school fine arts, who are clean and well fed, or who behave nicely every day. If that's what you're expecting, public education leadership is not the place for you. We are here to promote the success of *all* students. If that isn't what you have in mind, there are jobs available all over the United States outside of education. Find one, and enjoy it. We need committed souls, passionate about creating success in the lives of every student. This is the philosophy on which public education is built. It is certainly the philosophy on which these standards were founded.

Philosophical Framework

Now to the specifics of Standard 1. This one is all about vision. Above all else, if we do not have an identified, targeted vision of excellence for our schools, then who will have it? I am glad that this is Standard 1 because it sets the stage for all the others. How can we talk about curriculum, instruction, student learning, school organization, operations, or resources if we have no idea what direction or with what specific plan we are to apply them?

There are people who do not put emphasis on a school vision or mission. Like culture and climate, they consider vision and mission merely the "soft stuff" that people in ivory towers talk about but that have no real meaning in the actual management of a school. Well, guess what? If we do not know where or why we're going someplace, it should come as no surprise when we don't get there. We must "begin with the end in mind" (Covey, 1990a). Think of your campus vision as the ultimate destination on a major trip you are planning. There are four steps you must take to get there: development, articulation, implementation, and stewardship of the vision.

First, you have to collaboratively decide where it is you are going with your travel companions. If one person is planning a trip to London, someone else has his or her heart set on Rome, and still another person really wants to go to Lake Tahoe, then there's a problem. How can you book flights to all those places at the same time? You cannot. It's imperative that everyone sits down, talks about it, and decides together where it is you'll all be going. This does not mean the other locations aren't good destinations or that you won't go there another time. It just means that this time, you have decided collectively to go somewhere else. This stage of the process is *the development of the vision*. It involves getting faculty, staff members, families, and committee members together to talk, discuss, collaborate, and use data-driven decision making to determine exactly where the campus is now and where it wants to be in the future. The place the school wants to be becomes the campus vision. From this point on, everything the campus does should be aligned with that vision. Develop goals and strategies to achieve it. Align resources and staff development with it. Everything said, done, planned for, or purchased should focus on the achievement of this collaboratively developed campus vision. This does not mean the vision won't change as the school changes. It simply means that at this moment in time, this is the school's vision. As times and situations transition, so will the vision. Everything grows and changes. So does the vision.

Articulation of the vision is when we begin to communicate it. Articulation is vital; without it, the rest of the school community has no idea what the vision is. It is critically important that everyone be a part of the plan. Everyone must take part in developing it to be able to articulate and communicate it effectively. If we plan a trip but do not tell others when and where we are going, they cannot help us get there; they can't find us or come to our aid in case of an emergency. In schools, we must communicate to everyone—parents, community members, civic clubs, churches, strangers on the street—who we are, what we are there for, where we are going, what our plans are. Then we must invite them to join us in our crusade. Everyone involved with or who has an interest in the school is a part of the school community. The difference between success and failure revolves around analyzing and solving problems to overcome any barrier to success. We need everyone in the community to help us achieve our vision.

To achieve the vision demands more than articulation. Still more talking, discussing, and brainstorming from the school community is a must. The same is true with the next step in the process of making the vision a reality: *implementation of the vision.* We need everyone involved and empowered. People support what they help to build. Nothing in life is successful if multiple stakeholders do not share and support it. There is no such thing as blind luck. If we are to dream big dreams, set high standards, and develop idealistic visions of how

Figure 3.1

schools could be versus how they actually are today, then we need all the help we can get in developing, articulating, and implementing the goals and strategies necessary for success. Figure 3.1 shows the alignment of the components necessary to achieve the campus or district vision.

Specific, detailed goals and strategies to achieve the vision must be identified. All campus, grade, or content area goals should point toward and be aligned with the campus vision. Likewise, all campus activities—whether curricular, co-curricular, extracurricular, or per-taining to professional development—should also be aligned with achievement of at least one goal. Carrying this further, everything in the campus budget should also be targeted toward campus activities, goals, and achievement of the campus vision. The opposite is also true. All resources necessary, including time management, must be identified and included in the campus budget. Assessment must be integrated to ensure accountability of progress toward goal attain-ment, as illustrated in Figure 3.2.

What gets measured gets done. It is as simple as that. Therefore, all activities, instructional strategies, curriculum planning, and so forth should always have an assessment component to guarantee that progress is being made. If it is not, it's time to modify or get rid of that strategy or activity. Develop and implement new ones that are more productive, cost-efficient, or both. All of this is part of imple-menting the shared campus vision. Without implementation, we are all talk and no action. Talk without action gets us nowhere. We are past the point of going nowhere in education. It is time for action. Implementation of the collaboratively developed vision is action.

The principal and other school leaders also must take responsi-bility for a fourth step in the process of achieving the vision. Stewardship of the vision is a point in the process when even effec-tive schools can falter. Some school leaders can handle the arti-culation and implementation of the vision because these things are relatively concrete. You develop a plan for implementation and

Figure 3.2

success, communicate it well, solicit buy-in, and work the plan. Then you start over and continually repeat the process over and over until the vision is reached. Everything is cyclical in nature and in education.

But stewardship of the vision is much harder. It is difficult to sustain momentum once it has been generated. Everyone has heard about flash-in-the-pan ideas for school improvement that survive only a short time or, worse, new bandwagon ideas that are supposed to solve all the problems in education—and society, too, while they're at it. All sorts of people and districts jump on the bandwagon, pouring money, effort, time, and other resources into the idea and then are disappointed when early formative results do not support original predictions. There is significant danger in premature summative evaluations before time and true assessment in multiple forms can take place. Bandwagon leadership is dangerous. This is why it takes so much time during the early, formative stages to talk, discuss, and develop a vision that truly represents your specific school. If not, it is doomed to failure, often taking you with it. Failure is not a good thing and does nothing to support the cause of public education in a democratic society. There are no magical, bandwagon answers to the problems facing education today. The real solutions for moving our schools forward only come with deep reflection, insight, study, and analysis of multiple sources of data. Every campus goal, strategy, and activity should be based on this type of in-depth synthesis. Only this deep reflective analysis will help the leader become a true steward of the campus vision. No one is successful all the time. No school is successful every day. We all make mistakes. A true steward of the vision is always there to encourage others and themselves to get back up when they fall down. Falling down and making mistakes, personally or professionally, only proves we are human. It takes real guts to pick yourself up, dust yourself off, and start all over again, but this is the only way your school will ever reach its vision.

Development, articulation, and implementation of the vision create synergy. Stakeholders become motivated and energized. But over time, fatigue and reality can discourage the heartiest of educators. This is why being a steward of the vision is so important. It is the principal's responsibility to support, nurture, and sustain the vision of the school in good times and bad, to encourage people when they are down, and to keep everyone focused on attaining the vision of success built together.

In summary, to promote the success of all students, as principals and other school leaders, it is our responsibility to "facilitate the development, articulation, implementation, and stewardship of a school or district vision of learning." Facilitate does not mean dictate. Facilitate means to provide for and enable others to be able to attain their goals. But we cannot stop there. We must see to it that this vision is "shared and supported by the school community." To reiterate, people support what they help to build. From beginning to end, Standard 1 flows toward the end result of a campus or district vision of excellence for all learners. It embodies a campus culture and climate of collaborative leading, sharing, and decision making. It empowers others in the process of developing, articulating, implementing, and being stewards of a campus vision that makes us stretch to reach it while supporting each other along the way. Together we can do it. Go forth now and make it happen. Then be the world's most diligent and prudent steward of your school's vision of excellence for every child.

Below are three case studies that are examples of specific components of Standard 1. They are followed by open-ended questions and suggested professional growth activities. Remember, the amount of benefit people get out of anything is directly proportional to the amount of effort they put into it. Therefore, take your time as you read and study these scenarios, questions, and suggested activities. They are not designed for light reading, but for sincere reflection, analysis, and application. Keep in mind the words of Covey (1990b), who said that one habit of an effective person is to "seek first to understand." Read and study now as you "seek first to understand" the goals a standards-based principal must pursue.

CASE STUDIES

Development and Articulation of the Vision: Empowering the Learning Community to Develop the Campus Vision

Upon being assigned as principal of Romper Elementary School, Mary Lynn Watson discovered significant differences in academic performance among some of the campus subgroups. She learned that campus morale was low because district officials had targeted it as needing significant improvement. Ms. Watson knew the first step she must take was to facilitate the development of a collectively developed campus vision. She then planned to help coordinate activities to facilitate the school in setting goals and defining the techniques necessary to meet them. In addition, she had a strong desire to increase parental and community involvement in the school, thus creating a true learning community in which everyone worked collaboratively.

Ms. Watson began the year with open discussions pertaining to the development of the vision, inviting faculty and staff, parents, and interested community members to take part. Committees were formed with members of the campus-based decision-making team serving as coordinators. Through this process, stakeholders in the campus developed a vision of where they wanted their school to go academically. This included increasing parental involvement in the success of all students and finding strategies that would motivate parents and other community members to become actively involved in the school. Ms. Watson empowered individuals within the public arena to have a voice in the direction the campus was taking and selecting the steps to get there by involving them in the decision-making process, promoting collaboration, and facilitating ownership in both the vision and the school. By not making top-down, directive decisions but empowering the stakeholders of the school community, Ms. Watson was able to plant seeds for shared stewardship of the school vision that she would continue to nurture throughout the year.

Reflective Analysis: Pause and Think

1. Although the vast preponderance of the faculty and staff support the new campus vision, there is a handful that does not. What could be done to address this situation?

2. Because the campus has been targeted by the district for improvement, some parents would like to transfer their children to schools with better academic records. What steps should be taken to address this issue?

3. Although district administrators have given you a directive to improve student performance, once they hear some of the planned campus strategies and activities, they raise a few concerns. In this situation, what should the principal do as the liaison between the campus and central administration?

4. As facilitator of the development and articulation of a school vision of learning at a campus where some demographic subgroups were not performing well academically, what steps would you take to target improvement?

5. Identify obstacles to effective communication and attempts at change. What could you do to address these issues?

6. What steps would you take to sustain and nurture the vision once it is articulated?

Implementation and Stewardship of the Vision: Disaggregation of Data to Implement the Campus Vision

Simon Martin is principal of Robert Graham Middle School. Last year, his campus barely missed being named a Blue Ribbon School. This year, he and the campus are committed to Graham attaining this distinguished designation. Although student scores on standardized tests are high, the Campus Improvement Committee is determined to see them go higher. Working closely with Mr. Martin, the committee undertook the enormous task of breaking down the scores of every student in the school by subject and concept and by students' race, gender, and socioeconomic group to look for trends and to identify strengths and weaknesses. They solicited help from all faculty and staff to create ownership in the process and the results. They made plans to address identified areas that needed improvement by subject, concept, and individual needs. Benchmark practice tests were given midyear, and those results were also disaggregated and analyzed. Meetings were held every 2 weeks as teachers sought to work together to integrate concepts and better address student needs. Parent volunteers were solicited during the final weeks before testing to reinforce targeted concepts. Other community members provided support for teachers and staff by taking care of many of the little things that take time away from teaching and learning. The entire learning community worked together to address the individual needs of all students at Robert Graham Middle School.

Reflective Analysis: Pause and Think

1. Describe Mr. Martin's role in helping Graham become a Blue Ribbon School.

2. Describe the positives and negatives of utilizing parents and other community members in classrooms. What can be done to turn the negatives into positives?

3. Describe specific ways to involve parents in the day-to-day operation of the school if they do not feel they have anything to offer or if their primary language is not English.

4. Compare and contrast the utilization of teachers collaborating for the success of all students at Graham Middle School versus collaboration—or lack of collaboration—at your current campus. What could be done differently or better within your organization?

5. There are teachers who would not wish to individualize lessons according to the needs of every student. In what ways could you proactively encourage them to do so?

6. What should be done with a teacher who flatly refuses to do anything beyond putting in the minimum effort required for teaching and learning?

Community Involvement: A Voice for ESL (English as a Second Language) Families

Maurini Reyes is principal of Emily Smith Early Childhood Center. Her campus serves students in pre-kindergarten through second grade. A large segment of the population is Hispanic. Many of the students do not speak English; have never been to school; have never held a crayon, pencil, or scissors; and have not been read to in either Spanish or English. The campus has collaborated with the community to secure local and federal grants to work with parents. They seek to actively bring parents into the school community through literacy outreach programs. Civic clubs, churches, and businesses have donated money, goods, and time to benefit the outreach efforts of the school. Ms. Reyes and her campus team have developed and implemented activities such as programs to teach parents to speak and read English or to use computers, to help them obtain U.S. citizenship or prepare for the General Equivalency Diploma test, and to learn and practice parenting skills. Specific classes are offered to show parents how to help their children develop reading and mathematical skills. Supplemental early-childhood programs are available for infants and toddlers, as is babysitting so that parents can attend day or evening classes. Ms. Reyes believes that as the school reaches out to the community at large—and to families in particular—students will benefit. She seeks ways to incorporate the community in the success of the Emily Smith Early Childhood Center.

Reflective Analysis: Pause and Think

1. Describe the types of planning necessary to develop and fund programs such as those at Emily Smith Early Childhood Center.

2. Why is it necessary to have family outreach programs? What impact should these programs ultimately have on students?

3. What other things could Ms. Reyes consider to enhance learning opportunities for parents and students at her school?

4. In what other ways could Ms. Reyes solicit community support?

5. What effects, if any, do external support such as grants, goods, services, and time have on student achievement? Considering the growing red tape associated with federal compliance issues, is it worth the effort to solicit them?

6. In what ways could parents with limited English proficiency be utilized within the school setting?

7. Describe the connection between poverty and the lack of student experience. Can one exist without the other? How? What can be done to bridge these gaps?

ACTIVITIES FOR PROFESSIONAL DEVELOPMENT

The principal should

- Plan staff development concentrating on the concept of vision and on brainstorming activities regarding the development, articulation, implementation, and evaluation of the campus's own vision
- Plan off-campus retreats to facilitate teambuilding and provide time to focus in-depth on the campus vision and specific strategies to obtain it
- Invite teachers, community members, and administrators from other campuses inside or outside the district to share stories of how they successfully addressed similar situations
- Organize fieldtrips to observe other campuses undergoing similar circumstances successfully
- Provide follow-up time for discussion, analysis, and application planning after attending lectures by guest speakers or participating in other growth opportunities

- Develop and implement various community-oriented activity nights on campus pertaining to issues relevant to parents and other stakeholders. Provide on-campus babysitting for younger children, possibly provided by secondary-student group clubs from feeder schools
- Provide training in site-based decision-making, consensus-building, and conflict-resolution skills for the school community
- Provide staff development on basic and alternative models of assessment, how to disaggregate and analyze test scores and other forms of measurement, and how to use the results for enhanced teaching and learning
- Provide opportunities for "Book Talk" sessions at which faculty and staff members, after reading targeted books related to specific campus needs, discuss the issues raised and how they relate to the campus and brainstorm ways to benefit the school (serve light refreshments)
- Facilitate the contributions of community members from diverse backgrounds to talk to the faculty and staff about cultural differences as well as their subtle and not-so-subtle nuances related to schools and society today
- Facilitate discussion and analysis of ways to address, appreciate, and respond to cultural differences in the school environment

Conclusions

In this chapter, we have discussed Standard 1 in detail. We know that an effective principal supports the success of every student in every facet of his or her life. In so doing, the principal facilitates the development, articulation, implementation, and stewardship of a vision of learning that is shared and supported by everyone involved. There was nothing in this chapter to indicate that this is an easy task. It is not. It requires intense caring, commitment, passion, and perseverance. It involves picking ourselves up when we are physically and emotionally drained and doing likewise for others. It is pressing on against all odds toward an identified vision of excellence and overcoming obstacles to success. It means never, ever giving up. In the case studies, we witnessed how principals working with different types of populations toward entirely different goals had common characteristics of caring, commitment, passion, and perseverance. You have seen Standard 1 applied from different perspectives in varying situations. Now let's see how you do on your own.

The Ultimate Application

1. Describe the process you would undertake for creating a vision statement with ownership from all stakeholders in the learning community.

2. Prepare a potential vision statement for your organization.

3. Once the vision is developed, in what ways would you facilitate its articulation and communication within the learning community?

4. Why is it important for campus goals to be developed collaboratively by the learning community instead of by the principal alone?

5. Compare and contrast schools with and without an identified and targeted vision. In real terms, what would the differences be, if any?

6. What are the differences between a campus vision and campus goals?

7. Describe and discuss the importance of alignment of the campus vision and goals with curriculum, instruction, assessment, resources, budgets, and staff professional development.

8. Create a case study that demonstrates the alignment process.

CHAPTER FOUR

Reaching for the Stars

Creating a Culture That Values Enhanced Performance

STANDARD 2:

A school administrator is an educational leader who promotes the success of all students by advocating, nurturing, and sustaining a school culture and instructional program conducive to student learning and staff professional growth.

Once the vision of the school has been developed, articulated, implemented, and is in the continuous process of being maintained, a culture of high expectations and performance has been established. Now it is important that all stakeholders continue to support this vision. This leads directly into Standard 2. In this standard, the educational leader continues to promote the success of all students by advocating, nurturing, and sustaining the school culture that has been developed through the goals, expectations, culture, climate, and values surrounding the vision.

PHILOSOPHICAL FRAMEWORK

Culture

Whereas climate has been described as the way things feel within an organization, culture—a term originally used by archeologists—refers to the way things are done within the society (Thomson, 1993). Together the culture and climate of an organization create a powerful conception of what the organization values, of what its expectations are, and of the image it projects. Schools, as organizations, fall within these parameters. How many times have you walked onto a campus and within minutes sensed that it is a good place, a place where everyone is valued, where students come first, and where people are fulfilled by work? That is climate. It is the spirit or the "feel" of the school. Have you ever walked onto another campus and, again within minutes, had the sensation of "What's going on around here?," "Who's running this ship?," or "What *is* this? A concentration camp?" Unfortunately, that's climate, too. You decide which type you prefer. Then decide which climate you think best exemplifies a culture that is worth advocating, nurturing, and sustaining. That is the culture to which Standard 2 refers.

The three words *advocating, nurturing,* and *sustaining* are important to the lifeblood of the school. As described in Standard 1, advocating, nurturing, and sustaining are keys to the stewardship of the vision. Once the vision has been developed and implemented, specific goals and the strategies to achieve them are collaboratively developed (Wilmore, 2002). Things begin to happen. At first, we take baby steps forward. Every one of them should be celebrated and rewarded (Deal & Peterson, 1994, 1999; Thomson, 1993; Wilmore, 2001). Nothing is too small to celebrate. This doesn't mean the school turns into one big party. It means that what gets recognized, gets reinforced. We want to reinforce positive behaviors and progress toward the vision. Progression can be achieved through little things. The important point is to let the school community know the principal noticed, recognized, reinforced, and was pleased to see this happen. In these ways, the principal encourages and nurtures appropriate strategies for creating a positive school culture.

In doing these things, the principal goes beyond advocating a school culture and instructional program that is focused on growth. The principal becomes a nurturer of the entire school community, the shepherd of the flock, the person who provides the sustaining lifeblood and passion to the school. Think of a wonderful field that is cultivated and planted with the best of intentions; if it does not receive life-sustaining water, it will wither and die. Similarly, a school culture without nurturance of its values will meet a similar fate. The school will revert to the status quo bureaucracy it was before the collaborative process began. It is up to the principal to facilitate a learning community that values the heritage, culture, values, and diversity of the school and community—including language, disabilities, gender, race, and socioeconomic status. It is up to the principal to be the leader in providing the stimulus of continuous improvement through campus improvement plans and creative action research projects that are practitioner-friendly but can have amazing results (Glanz, 1998). It is the principal that gets the ball rolling and who is also the person primarily responsible for sustaining its motion.

This doesn't mean that the principal is the only person with responsibility. It is up to everyone to nurture and support each other, sustain the vision, enrich the culture, and see to it that all students have every opportunity to grow, learn, and succeed. It is up to the principal to set a level of expectations such that obstacles are things that merely get in the way of success, but do not stop it. It is up to the principal to encourage others when they are down and to help pick them up again.

The rest of the school community must do the same for the school. Because, in the end, the principal is simply a human being, showing up for work every day, trying to do his or her best to make the world a better place—starting with one school. The principal, being human, will make mistakes. In a nurturing and sustaining culture, everyone involved will help and support everyone else, creating a team. When one person succeeds, everyone succeeds. When another person is less than successful, everyone else works together to find a better way to address the issue. But, most of all, in an advocating, nurturing, and sustaining school culture, no one ever gives up. To give up is to take your eyes off the vision. We must keep our eyes on a vision of pure excellence and never, ever give up. Our schools deserve nothing less.

Instructional Programs

The instructional program is the primary focus of all this energy, passion, and commitment. It is the basic distinction between school leadership and any other type of organizational leadership. Curriculum and instruction are the fundamental purpose—the "meat and potatoes"—of what makes schools unique (Wilmore, 2002). Whereas the campus vision is global and relates to every aspect of school life, goals are more specific. They are the definite benchmarks that must be achieved to reach the vision. They will fall in various categories and will vary with every school and situation. Therefore it is critically important that each school community work collaboratively to develop goals that meet their individual needs. There is no such thing as a generic or cookie-cutter goal. There should be goals that relate to designing, implementing, and evaluating all forms of curriculum, instruction, programs, products, *and* personnel. There should be other goals promoting technology and information systems that accommodate diverse student needs. Goals and strategies to achieve them should incorporate principles of effective instruction, research, research methods, and other resources including professional literature, school and district data, and other relevant information. Multiple types of data from various sources must always be used to eliminate premature or incorrect decisions and to minimize bias.

For as many schools as there are in the United States, there should be that many different sets of goals. There should be campus goals, grade-level goals, subject- or content-related goals, counseling and advising goals, cocurricular goals, and extracurricular goals. There should be goals relating to every facet of the instructional program. When one is reached, new ones should be developed. There should always be goals. John Hoyle of Texas A&M University says, "There is a funny thing about people who set goals. They tend to reach them" (Hoyle, English, & Steffy, 1998). This is part of the sustenance of the school culture and instructional program conducive to student learning.

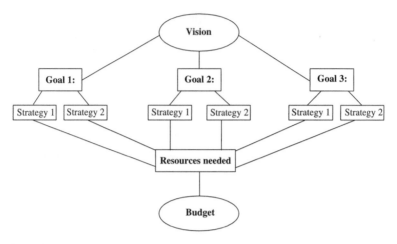

Figure 4.1

The same is true for organizations and individuals on the professional and the personal levels. All organizations and people should have goals on all levels. There will be big goals and smaller goals. The thing they have in common is that little goals always point toward larger goals, and larger goals always point toward the campus vision of excellence—where we want our school to be rather than where we actually are. This vision should be reflected in every aspect of the school. This concept should be so far reaching that every element of the campus budget can be directly correlated with the vision (Wilmore, 2002), as shown in detail in Figure 4.1.

The same is true on a personal level. Every goal each person identifies on the professional level should be ultimately aimed at enhancing student achievement. On the personal level, goals should help us achieve our own identified mission, otherwise our we are not focused on our life's work. Something doesn't feel quite right. Covey (1990b) says it is important for each person to have an identified mission statement, a synthesis of what we hope to achieve and by what means. He says we should regularly audit our daily activities to see if what we are actually spending our time doing is in alignment and congruence with our mission. When this is not happening, it explains why any person becomes unhappy or frustrated. Then it's time to make changes, to improve the situation, and to bring our lives back in congruence with our ultimate purpose (Covey, 1990a, 1990b, 1994).

Student Learning

The same is true with campus goals. To achieve them, we must have specific and detailed curricular and instructional plans that focus on student learning and success. These will include varying types of curriculum, instruction, and assessment that are based on developmental, learning, and motivational theories. It does not mean that one method is better than another. It means that in meeting the needs of different learners with various cultural backgrounds, experiences, and learning modalities, we will need to find the appropriate strategies that work for this learner. This will include studying subgroup demographic data to discern strengths and weaknesses within groups and for individuals. But it goes beyond numbers. It requires getting to know students as individual people in addition to statistics, finding out what works to enhance their learning and then applying it. This is a lot more work than the average lesson plan, which usually provides for every student to do the same thing at the same time as everyone else, regardless of whether the activities are relevant or meaningful to his or her needs or life context. It often does not provide for individual differences or learning styles. This works for some students, but we shouldn't wonder why so many students drop out, become disrespectful, create a ruckus, or are bored to death. When learning is authentic and relevant, students will become engaged in the process. When this happens, the rest is history. They are interested and connected, and they will learn.

The type of instructional strategy really makes no difference. We must be willing to take risks and embrace change for the purpose of engaging one student at a time and providing an avenue to success that was not there before. Too many students turn off rather than turn on to what we offer because it does not meet their needs or circumstances. We have to think outside the box, to step out of our comfort zones, and take risks (Blanchard & Bowles, 1998; Johnson, 1998; Sergiovanni, 1992, 1996, 2000; Wilmore, 2002) to find ways to help students who almost slipped through the cracks. The point is that we must study every aspect of student data to individualize and focus on the individual rather than think how lucky the student is to get to come to school and spend the days with us. A lot of them really don't think so. What are we going to do about it?

Professional Growth

I cannot overemphasize the value of goal setting for professional growth. We discussed it in relation to vision, campus improvement, student learning, and personal as well as professional growth. We discussed Stephen Covey and his strong belief in searching for and identifying your personal mission statement. Sometimes just doing that answers a lot of questions and ambiguities in our lives. It is no wonder some people are not happy; they aren't pursuing their own mission because they haven't identified it. Does this mean that what they are doing is not worthwhile? Not necessarily. Does it mean that the mission they are meant to pursue is better than the journey they are now undertaking? Definitely not. It just means that different people have varying purposes in life. One person's purpose is not better or of greater value than another's. Together we create a whole. Each of us is needed to help make this world a better place, one individual at a time. We all have purpose. The real issue is to find individual purpose and then pursue it vigorously. Finding our purpose and then developing strategies and techniques to achieve it are essential components in the development of professional growth plans. Everyone should have a plan. Principals must model this behavior for the learning community by developing, implementing, and assessing their own. This is letting your walk match your talk and being a true role model.

Within the field of education, there are many different avenues for people to pursue. Sometimes other people can see something in us that we cannot see. Plant the seeds of professional development in others. You never know which ones will take root.

- "Have you ever thought about going into administration? You would make a wonderful principal. You are a natural leader."
- "Become a counselor? No, I never thought about it. But now that you bring it up, you may have a point. Yes, I think maybe

I would be interested in checking into what it would take for me to become a counselor."

- "Maybe I should pursue an ESL certification. We are getting more and more students at our campus whose native language is not English. I feel frustrated because I do not feel equipped to meet their needs. If I go back to school and study strategies to help students acquire language skills, I could use those skills with all my students. Yes, that really is a good idea."

- "Ms. Townzen always seems to have such good ideas to stimulate the higher-level thinking skills of her students. Her students seem to really enjoy her classes, and they do so well. She took some night classes at the university on stimulating creativity. In fact, I think she said something about taking a class on learning differences online. Maybe I will check into doing something like that too. Maybe that would be fun. I could use a boost. Maybe Ms. Townzen had a point when she asked me to do that with her."

When you plant a seed, you never know if it will root. Sometimes it doesn't happen right away. It takes a while. As principals, we are on a constant quest to develop every person to his or her highest potential to promote achievement. The principal is charged with the responsibility of facilitating professional growth plans and development activities for all members of the learning community. Doing this with each person enhances the productivity of the entire organization. John Maxwell makes a stirring case for the development of subordinates in his book *Developing the Leaders Around You* (1995). The best way to carry the momentum of the organization forward is to fill it with the best people available, then empower them to do what they needs to be done to reach the community's goals.

The last thing we want is a stagnant, status quo school. If your school is not moving forward, it is standing still. Still water becomes stagnant. We do not have time to stand still or have stagnant schools. There are students, families, and communities all around us that need help. There are people who need to learn how to read or how to use a calculator or computer. Others need to learn basic literacy, mathematical, and technological skills. Still others need to find out where to find basic community services; how to get a GED; how to select a college and apply for admission or financial assistance; how to apply for food stamps, welfare, free or reduced lunch, and so forth. As members of our learning community, these individuals deserve to grow. We are charged with the responsibility of facilitating that growth.

The list goes on and on. There is no time to stand still. Our goal is straightforward: We are here to facilitate each person in the learning community in identifying and pursuing his or her dreams, turning them into reality, and promoting sound, research-based instructional methods that enhance teaching and learning. Our goal is to provide whatever support is necessary to encourage our teachers and staff to set high personal and professional goals and then do whatever is necessary to reach them. For you see, when one of us succeeds, we all succeed. We are a team. We are a family. Together we grow. Together we achieve. Together we are powerful. Alone we are small. Together we can change the world.

What are your dreams? What are your goals? Goals without deadlines are only dreams (Wilmore, 2002). Take time right now to identify what you would love to do if you were guaranteed success. Stop a minute. Visualize yourself doing whatever that is beautifully. Nice feeling, isn't it? Now what do you need to do or change in your life to see to it that what you visualized becomes reality? Do it. Do not let anything or anyone stand in your way. In doing this, whether it directly relates to education or not, you will become a better you. When that happens, the natural progression is that you become a happier, more productive educator. Is that not what professional growth is all about?

In summary, we have talked about the principal as the primary, but not the only, person responsible for advocating, nurturing, and sustaining a school culture and instructional program conducive to student learning and staff professional growth. We have stressed the importance of setting personal and professional goals for every arena of life in the form of professional growth plans, facilitating the same process in others, and using research-based curriculum and instruction that enhance the learning of every student regardless of context or circumstance. We discussed planning growth activities that focus on individualizing for the unique interests and needs of every student, even though we realize this will entail a great deal of hard work. We understand this is asking a lot from all of us, but we know that to move mountains, we have to take the first step. We have emphasized the importance of never settling for the status quo because we do not want to become stagnant. Our world does not have time for that.

We know that it is up to us as educational leaders to lead the crusade and advocate for the education of every student and family. To do that, we will have to take risks and embrace change. We know this is often an unsettling experience and that not all members of the community are cut out for it. This doesn't mean they are failures. It means they have a different calling. Maybe education isn't a perfect fit for them. As for us, we are on a continuing quest to change the world, one student at a time.

Following are four case studies that address Standard 2 and the issues of culture, instructional programs, student learning, and professional growth. Each is followed by open-ended questions designed to make you think. Thinking hard could make you step out of your comfort zone. Are you ready to do that? If so, read on.

CASE STUDIES

Culture: Celebrating Success!

Joe Redding is principal of Arthur Stillwell Elementary School, a K–5 campus. It is important to Joe that Stillwell have a demonstrated culture that values and celebrates success for all learners. He knows that for the rest of the learning community to incorporate these principles into everyday life, he must make sure his walk matches his talk. Although time-consuming, Joe seeks to be a role model for his faculty and staff in valuing and celebrating student success both academically and behaviorally. He feels the time he invests in this proactive, developmental manner will pay off in the lives of faculty, students, and families at a later date. To that end, he regularly visits classrooms and becomes a participant in learning, working with students and teachers, helping students in need, working with them independently, and teaching lessons. He encourages teachers to send students who have accomplished a difficult task to his office for praise such that visits to the principal's office are not restricted to students with problems. He particularly stresses success in reading in the early grades. He encourages first-grade teachers to send students who are having difficulty learning to read to him. When they are successful, they celebrate together, calling home to let the children share the success with their parents. Together Joe and these children create an award using PowerPoint, announcing what book the student read aloud. The student takes the award home to showcase his or her accomplishment. Joe follows up, praising students for their efforts and achievements, even if they are incrementally small. Joe believes triumph is built on success and encourages a "can-do" spirit and culture within the Stillwell learning community.

Joe exemplifies the same values with students who are having difficulty maintaining appropriate behavior in the classroom. He targeted five fifth-grade boys who were creating havoc and then worked with them, their teachers, their counselor, and their parents to help develop behavior modification plans. He meets with them regularly to discuss their small steps forward and provides immediate reinforcement. When the boys have a successful week, he spends 30 minutes on Friday afternoons playing basketball with them. The boys look forward to this positive interaction with their principal. Although they are not successful each week, the idea of basketball with the principal is a positive motivator toward behavior modification. When they have not been individually or collectively successful, he still meets with them at the end of the week to discuss their behavior. He asks them what went wrong and poses other insightful questions. He has them identify ways they could have better handled the situations and ways they can improve during the following week.

In both the academic and behavioral arenas, Joe Redding seeks to cultivate a culture that values and celebrates success for all students at Stillwell Elementary. His goal is for every student to leave Stillwell equipped academically and emotionally to handle the new challenges of intermediate school. The time he spends demonstrating his belief in a culture that values success regardless of the issue is a seed sown toward his faculty and staff demonstrating the same values, thus multiplying the efforts toward—and ultimately the rewards of—all people succeeding.

Reflective Analysis: Pause and Think

1. Is Joe Redding an instructional leader? Why or why not?

2. Mr. Redding invests a great deal of time on personal interaction with students and teachers. He has been criticized for not spending enough time in the office. In his situation, how would you respond to this criticism and why?

3. Why is it important for principals to become involved with students on a personal level?

4. How could this interaction result in fewer disciplinary referrals?

5. Describe ways you can become more actively involved in the individual lives of students on your campus.

6. Describe an ideal school culture that enhances student performance. Compare and contrast it with what currently exists on your campus.

7. Describe ways you could improve the culture of success at your school.

8. Why is it important to involve collaborative planning, implementation, and assessment of campus-culture-enhancing strategies within the learning community?

9. Campus culture is often directly linked with learning community morale. In what ways could this be assessed? For what purposes and with what effects?

Instructional Program: Differing Instructional Philosophies

Cornelius Anthony is principal of Eisenhower Charter School, a publicly funded charter school geared toward an elementary at-risk student population. Cornelius was impressed with a specific scripted reading program. Without the input of others, he implemented the program during the previous school year. During the first year, there was skepticism among some faculty about using a totally scripted reading program. They felt this removed their autonomy and creativity as teachers and also severely restricted the students' access to a variety of instructional methods and literature. At the end of the year, however, standardized test results did show improvements in most reading concepts.

Mr. Anthony was greatly encouraged by the results of these tests. However, these results did little to abate the resentment of teachers who felt multiple assessment tools should be used to ascertain student growth. As resentment grew, Mr. Anthony spent considerable funds to provide additional training and organize fieldtrips for faculty members to see the program in action at other schools. As the second year of the program began, teachers became more vocal in expressing their dislike for the program and their resentment toward the principal for pushing a curriculum on them without considering their differing instructional philosophies. At the same time, Mr. Anthony became more defensive of the program, continually pointing to the standardized test results as evidence of its success.

Reflective Analysis: Pause and Think

1. What type of leadership style is Mr. Anthony displaying? With what results?

2. A tenuous working relationship now exists between the principal and staff. Describe what Mr. Anthony should do to build consensus, improve relationships, and generate a positive instructional focus and culture.

3. In what ways could this difference in philosophy have been addressed before the program was implemented?

4. Is the principal being dictatorial? Why or why not? Justify your position.

5. Are the teachers being contentious? Why or why not? Justify your position.

6. If standardized test results show improvement in student scores, why are the teachers complaining?

7. In addition to a specific instructional strategy, what other factors should be considered in analyzing standardized test results?

8. Describe factors that are important in a well-rounded literacy program.

Student Learning: Changing Student Demographics

Jewel Matlock has been principal of Williamson Elementary for 25 years. She has seen the neighborhood change from a district in which doctors and other professionals were the predominant population to an area with a growing immigrant presence. The student population at Williamson has changed accordingly. Through the years, there has not been significant staff turnover at Williamson. Although most staff members have successfully adapted to the changing student population, some have not. In fact, there are staff members who openly refuse to address the differing needs of these students. They continue to teach with the same instructional strategies that have worked successfully in the past. Their view is that if these students want to succeed in the United States, they must learn English and adjust to the dominant cultural mores. Ms. Matlock is concerned about this attitude and wants to address it before it further affects student learning. Although many of the students are new to the United States, others have been at Williamson for several years and still have not mastered English. Another concern is that many of the new students who do not speak English are also low in language experiences in their native tongues. She facilitates the implementation of study groups to analyze the changing demographics at Williamson and how to best meet student needs.

Reflective Analysis: Pause and Think

1. Williamson Elementary is experiencing a philosophical divide between teachers who feel strongly that students should acclimate to the teaching styles of faculty versus those

who feel it is the faculty's responsibility to adapt to the needs of learners. As a team builder, how would you address this situation, resolve conflict, and take steps toward reaching a consensus while keeping the focus on what is best for the students?

2. Develop a plan to address the poor language acquisition of students at Williamson that includes parents, teachers, and other members of the school community.

3. Even within a single culture, there are basic philosophical differences regarding the effects of children learning an additional language and by what method(s) language acquisition should be taught. Many parents want their children to learn English but also express concern that they will lose contact with their own culture and heritage. As an educational leader, how would you address this philosophical issue?

4. What methods of assessment could be undertaken to discern why ESL students who have spent several years on campus have not yet learned English?

5. Some faculty at Williamson are experiencing difficulty dealing with change. What steps would you take to enhance appreciation for and response to changing student demographics and cultural needs that are both internal and external to the campus?

6. How important is shared vision in implementing change strategies within a school experiencing changing demographics?

7. How can parents be incorporated and integrated into the Williamson learning community and culture?

8. In what ways could students be utilized in the development of a new vision of excellence for Williamson Elementary?

9. There is a shortage of ESL-certified teachers in most areas. As a leader in staff professional development, outline a plan to address this concern for the benefit of all students and teachers on your campus.

Professional Growth: A Collaboratively Developed and Implemented Teacher Appraisal System

As principal of a private school for kindergarten through eighth grade, Elizabeth Jones is concerned about the lack of a consistent teacher appraisal system. The school is known for its excellent curriculum and a safe, orderly environment. Test results are good, and there is strong parental support for the campus. In the past, Elizabeth and her assistant principal have conducted nonsystematic visits in classrooms when they had time or when a need arose. Through professional reading and conference attendance, Elizabeth was convinced that the school would operate more productively for all students if a consistent appraisal system were in place. Although she has several ideas for components that the model should include, she feels the system would be better accepted by the faculty and ultimately of more value to them if they have significant input in its development. Because theirs is a private school, they have no state or district policies with which they must comply. They are free to develop a model that will work for their unique situation. In an open discussion before the beginning of the school year, Elizabeth expressed her appreciation for everyone's diligent work. She reminded the staff and faculty of the thoughts she shared with them the previous year about the development and implementation of an assessment system. She told them about the conferences she had attended over the summer and reported input from other principals with whom she had talked who did and did not use assessment systems.

Elizabeth told the faculty and staff that although they had an excellent school, nothing is ever perfect. An assessment system would provide feedback on ways they could improve and work together. She then opened the floor for discussion from everyone, telling them no decision had been made and that she valued their input. After considerable discussion over time, the faculty decided they would like to try an assessment system on a trial basis to see how it would work. Throughout the semester, teachers, parents, and others met to research and discuss ideas they wanted to incorporate into the assessment system. They discussed how the system would be implemented, how the results could be used, and ways the system could be evaluated.

Reflective Analysis: Pause and Think

1. Elizabeth Jones demonstrated a firm commitment to learning community input and empowerment. Such a strong commitment takes courage and confidence, qualities not all principals have. Describe potential pros and cons of providing such empowerment to others.

2. Ms. Jones broached the potentially controversial subject of a teacher appraisal system over a period of time rather than dropping it suddenly on the faculty. What benefits or disadvantages could such open disclosure procure?

3. Ms. Jones and her staff demonstrated high organizational maturity and health. In a school without these strengths, what safeguards should the principal employ when bringing up a controversial subject that needs significant learning community input?

4. Professional growth is an important component of all growing educators. What are some additional ways Ms. Jones could facilitate professional growth for her faculty, staff, and self?

5. Should safeguards be built in to the plan to ensure that teachers would not arbitrarily decide they want to discontinue the appraisal system because it was too stressful or they simply didn't like it? If so, what should these safeguards be?

6. Describe ways Ms. Jones could role model professional assessment of herself.

7. There is strong national discussion about whether student learning should be linked to teacher assessment. What is your position? Present research-based pros and cons for both sides of this issue.

8. If student learning were linked to teacher appraisal, what criteria should be used to ensure equity of opportunity for both students and staff members?

ACTIVITIES FOR PROFESSIONAL DEVELOPMENT

The principal should

- Appreciate that learning community members need adequate time to discuss the issue of campus culture and ways to enhance it
- Provide opportunities for learning community brainstorming to identify campus traditions and heritage and ways to celebrate these qualities
- Facilitate the development and implementation of a campus professional development needs assessment whereby input on campus training can be identified
- Facilitate plans to develop, fund, and implement results of the campus professional development needs assessment
- Coordinate the assessment and modification of curricular and instructional programs
- Supply resources necessary for developmentally appropriate curriculum and instruction
- Through multiple sources, provide training in timely advanced instructional strategies; topics may include benchmarking, diversity and cultural sensitivity, multilevel instruction, cooperative learning, curriculum and assessment alignment, vertical and horizontal teaming, problem solving, and conflict resolution, as well as literacy, mathematical, scientific, social science, fine arts, life skills approaches to enhance student learning and staff professional growth
- Provide time for learning community members to share their successes and concerns, to exchange ideas, to support each other, and to provide feedback in a safe environment
- Facilitate open, noncritical discussion of differing instructional models, techniques, and philosophical bases; positives and negatives to each approach; and ways to integrate the best of each approach to facilitate student learning and staff professional growth
- Provide opportunities for teachers to work in groups to brainstorm and share ideas that have been successful in working with students from other cultures and backgrounds or who have

limited English proficiency. Provide time for collaborative feedback toward piloting these ideas in other classrooms and evaluating results in a supportive manner to see what works and what does not

- Conduct personal formative and summative conferences with all members of the learning community to provide support and insight as they develop professional goals and identify strategies to reach them for the purposes of improved student learning and professional growth
- Arrange resources necessary to help teachers and other members of the learning community reach their goals and set new ones for continuous growth and opportunity
- Identify factors that relate to faculty and staff burnout; describe ways to nurture, sustain, and help them refocus on their individual missions as well as the vision and mission of the school
- Provide training and support for learning community members who work with at-risk students or others for whom school is not a pleasant experience

CONCLUSIONS

The Ultimate Application

1. Describe an ideal learning environment in which the principal advocates, nurtures, and sustains a school culture and instructional program that is conducive to student learning and staff professional growth.

2. Discuss the issue of school leaders involving the learning community in decision making. Synthesize the concepts, draw conclusions, and create possible applications.

3. Describe the attributes of school culture that you remember from the campus you attended as a child. Compare and contrast that with your school today. Whether positive or negative, draw conclusions and implications for school leadership.

4. Create a plan of specific ways you as an instructional leader can enhance student performance. Include a timeline and model of assessment.

5. Explain why it is important for principals to join professional organizations; participate in their meetings, conferences, and activities; and read professional literature.

6. Explain the benefits of educational leaders strongly encouraging members of their learning community to do likewise.

7. Describe the benefits of action research on a daily basis for active school improvement. Outline a project you could facilitate on your campus. Describe the purposes, steps, assessments, necessary resources, potential outcomes, and implications for improved teaching and learning.

CHAPTER FIVE

Steering the Ship

*Facilitating the Organization
and Operation of Learning
Community Resources*

STANDARD 3:

*A school administrator is an educational leader who
promotes the success of all students by ensuring management of the organization, operations, and resources
for a safe, efficient, and effective learning environment.*

S tandard 3 relates to the management and internal mechanisms
that facilitate the efficient running of an organization and that
enhance student learning. This encompasses all aspects of human
resource, facility, internal and external funding, technology, and
equipment management such that accountability to the public
is always above board. To incorporate and empower all stakeholders in the learning community, the leader must have excellent
communication and interpersonal skills such as conflict resolution,
consensus building, and group processes that are particularly
necessary when critical and divergent thinking is encouraged
and nurtured.

Philosophical Framework

Organization

There are administrators in many schools who have great vision and passion but, for whatever reason, cannot effectively facilitate the implementation of this vision and passion. They are great dreamers, but poor implementers. On the other hand, there are those who are great at paper-and-pencil tasks, are organized and efficient, and who could run the Library of Congress, but who have about as much passion as a toothpick. What we are looking for are great managers with magnificent vision and loads of passion and commitment to the school community. This isn't an easy combination to find. Locating people to lead our schools who are balanced managers and visionaries is quite a task, but one we are certainly up to.

Schools will not be successful having principals filled with passion and vision but who cannot make data-driven decisions based on facts and equity instead of presumption, bias, wrong information, or emotion. It does no good to aim for the moon but end up in court or fired because of decisions that were either illegal or outside district policy. Therefore, sound decision making is a top priority in leading an efficient school. Knowledge of research-based theories and concepts, and of local policies and state and federal laws, is essential for a successful administrator. They were developed for a reason: to provide a basic, equitable structure in which all schools should function. For example, if a disabled student moves from one district to another, federal law protects his or her rights to a free and appropriate public education. We cannot change an Individual Education Plan (IEP) just because we don't like it. If a change is necessary, it can only occur by consensus of an Admission, Review, and Dismissal (ARD) committee. Administrators cannot make sudden decisions on a whim because they think it is a good idea or because someone is on their back to take action. All decisions must be based on law and policy. Once those basic stipulations have been met, sound judgment, wisdom, and decision-making skills must be used. Usually, this is easier said than done.

Evaluation is an important component in making appropriate decisions regarding program assessment, continuation, modification, and cost-effectiveness, or if the program has served its purpose and it is time to end it. "How can we do it better?" should be the starting point for assessment of everything we do in schools. Nothing is exempt. It does not matter if we have lined up buses behind the cafeteria for 20 years. Is that the best place to line them up *now?* Is there a better or safer place *now*? Is there a better way to make algebra meaningful? Is there a better way to empower teachers? Is there a better way to involve parents and communities, modify curriculum, or improve instructional strategies? Is there a better way to do anything? Everything we do as administrators should be under continual assessment for better, more efficient, and less costly ways of accomplishing campus goals.

Sacred cows—programs that have been in existence for so long that no one can remember exactly when they began—are a problem. They are firmly entrenched in the school structure. No one can imagine not having them. Take, for example, computer labs. Is having multiple computers in one location and none anywhere else a prudent use of limited resources, including space? Or would students and learning be better served in a different arrangement? If so, what arrangement is that? Is the lab effective? Is it cost-efficient? Is it accessible? Could the same goals be accomplished in a more prudent, effective, or cost-efficient manner? In fact, are sacred cow programs achieving their goals at all?

Just because something has been done a certain way for a long time does not mean it cannot be improved with change. We must continually assess every aspect of our schools. Specific evaluative questions and criteria by which they will be appraised should be developed before the assessment begins. If everyone knows from formative stages what and how decisions will be made, confusion, hurt feelings, and mistrust can be avoided. Inefficient programs should not be allowed to continue just because they have been around forever or are someone's pet project. Do accurate, planned, and precise assessments. Base decisions on political, social, economic, legal, and cultural contexts and research-based data. Consider all perspectives and use multiple sources of data. Develop a reputation for being consistent, fair, ethical, and equitable to the three Ps of evaluation: personnel, programs, and products (Worthen, Sanders, & Fitzpatrick, 1996). In so doing, your school will function in an organized, orderly, efficient, and effective manner. Remember, a prime purpose of the school is to facilitate optimal student learning. This cannot be accomplished in a facility or organization that is disorganized, inconsistent, or unpredictable.

Operations

There is a distinction between organization and operations. Organization is the global oversight of sound judgment, data-driven decision making, and equity for all stakeholders on every issue resulting in safe, effective, and efficient schools. On the other hand, school operations focus on setting appropriate priorities to achieve campus goals. The entire learning community is not always going to agree happily on all issues, so the principal must have excellent communication and interpersonal skills as demonstrated by team and consensus building and conflict resolution. After skillfully led discussion and analysis, the school community must be able to identify and agree on basic, common values or indicators that will serve as benchmarks and keep everyone focused on campus vision. The principal must make sure that campus resources are also prioritized and aligned with the vision. Everything needed to implement strategies to reach prioritized goals and campus vision should be in the budget. The opposite is also true: There should not be anything in the budget that does not help the school attain its vision. If this is not the case, something is wrong. Either sufficient resources were not budgeted to accomplish a specific goal or expenses were more than what was predicted. With sound fiscal planning and proper alignment between campus goals and resources, this should not be an issue.

Internal and external communication skills are vital to the efficient operation of the school. Internal communication refers to articulation, discussion, and feedback inside the school. External communication refers to the same things outside the school. Similar to articulation of the vision, it does little good to have wonderful things happening at the school that no one knows about. One of the chronic problems with public education in the United States is that we do not do a good enough job to market the high-quality and unique things that are happening on our campuses. For so long, the public schools were virtually the only game in town. This is no longer true. Private, charter, and for-profit schools are on the rise across the country. There is also a large and growing population of home schooling. Because of federal laws ensuring every student an opportunity for a public education regardless of race, gender, religion, or disability, one can surmise that students who are enrolled in any other arenas are there because someone—either the student or the parents—decided public schools were not meeting students' needs. You have to ask yourself how this could happen if we are doing everything we should be. Would they make the same choice if they knew all their options within public education, if their concerns were being addressed, and if their children's needs were being met? Would there be a market for alternative educational opportunities if every public school treated their students as if their parents were paying tuition to have them there and thus felt they had voice in the direction the school was taking? What if every public school had a common and committed vision of the way they wanted to be instead of the way they are? What if every educator worked with vigor, energy, and passion toward that goal every day? What impact could we have on a truly free and democratic society for every child?

Communication inside and outside the school is imperative to the accomplishment of the school's goals as well as to the public image and perception of the school. Image starts at the top, with the principal. It filters down into all aspects of the school culture and climate. The attitudes and persona displayed by the principal have a direct effect on how the school is viewed, perceived, and responded to in the community. It is imperative that school leaders have a systematic plan for open, viable communication and collaboration inside and outside the school with staff, parents, and every other member of the learning community.

Resources

The issue of resource allocation is directly related to the organization and operation of the school for a safe, efficient, and effective learning environment. We will not make the world's best progress toward campus goals if we have no resources to help us achieve them. As previously stressed, necessary resources must be aligned with collaboratively developed long- and short-term campus goals. You cannot have one without the other, and this is why strategic planning is so important. In operational planning, we must think ahead to potential needs, possibilities, and problems that could arise, then make resource management decisions accordingly. Again, these should be data-driven decisions based on multiple sources of facts rather than presumptions or conjecture. Presumptions equate to biases, which often result in bad decisions.

With the shortage of tax dollars that most districts and schools face, virtually everyone is seeking external funding to supplement basic programs—and sometimes even to fund the basic needs of students. Federal funds, such as the Title programs, are always targeted, as are many state dollars based on similar formulas. But don't forget that corporations, businesses, foundations, civic clubs, churches, and even individuals are often willing to fund worthy projects if they are asked in an appropriate fashion and—let's face it—if the timing is right. There are so many groups in need of funds today that schools cannot be assured they'll be selected, but there are few groups that so obviously impact all strata of society as public school systems. It is always appropriate to have our eyes wide open and be on alert for alternative funding sources to provide additional resources for students and teachers and to facilitate student learning.

Finally, principals must have knowledge and be able to access and apply technological skills for all forms of school management from disciplinary referrals to budget maintenance and scheduling. There is no such thing as being able to ignore technological advances. It is as necessary in the school office as it is in the classroom. All principals must be technologically advanced and encourage others to be so as well. Technology and information systems have become an integral part of facilitating teaching and learning and of sound organizational management. The following are three case studies that highlight the educational leader's role in the organization, operations, and resource management of the campus.

CASE STUDIES

Organization: Shortcomings in Facilities and Resource Management

Rose Hill Academy is a public charter school beginning its second year of operation. Principal Wade Jones is quite concerned about several challenging situations. During the summer, the Board of Trustees contracted with an independent management firm to oversee the operation of the school and make sure it complies with all aspects of its state charter.

Rose Hill had a new facility scheduled to be ready for operation at the beginning of the school year. As construction continued, there were considerable delays, and the school was not ready for occupancy until after Christmas. The best space available for Rose Hill to use until their facilities were completed was leased from a local church. Unfortunately, there was considerably less square footage than what the school was expecting to have and than it had the previous year.

The budget was developed and the staff hired according to a projected average daily attendance of approximately 1,000 students. Because of the space shortage, less than half that number will be able to attend until the new facility opens. This will cause a considerable reduction in the amount of money the school will receive from the state. It has also caused confusion and distress among parents who had planned for their children to attend Rose Hill and among teachers and staff members who became concerned about their job security. The management firm assured the staff that their jobs were protected and that funds would be available through the interim period.

As school began, it became obvious that Rose Hill was financially unable to meet its budget. Expenditures were stripped to the minimum. By early October, 10 teachers and 5 paraprofessionals were faced with a Reduction in Force (RIF) situation, and there was a possibility of more layoffs in the future. Combined with the limited expenditures and space, this escalated the stress and low morale among faculty, staff, parents, and other learning community members.

While all this was taking place, Mr. Jones was informed that the management firm planned to implement various additional changes at Rose Hill that faculty felt were contrary to the vision of the school. A behavior management plan used at other schools they managed was to be put into place, students and staff would be required to wear uniforms, and a more prescriptive curriculum would be ordered as soon as funds became available. At this point, approximately 30% of the faculty and staff have resigned, and others are looking to leave as other employment becomes available.

Reflective Analysis: Pause and Think

1. Reflect on the actions of the management firm for Rose Hill and their effects on the principal. Describe his leadership role in this situation and make recommendations of additional things he could do.

2. What should the principal's first steps be to curb staff resignations?

3. Describe the components of an effective organizational management plan. Compare and contrast it with what occurred at Rose Hill.

4. Describe an appropriate organizational model that could be implemented to integrate facilities and budgetary shortfalls with the vision of the school.

5. Develop a flow chart of budgetary considerations and recommendations with which the learning community could be involved to facilitate conflict resolution as well as ownership in the problem, process, and resolution.

6. Describe factors that must be considered in staffing, budgeting, and student needs.

7. Develop a potential strategic organizational plan, created by the management firm, the principal, and the learning community that would address the immediate concerns at the school.

Operations: Crisis Management

The learning community at Lee Litchfield High School decided that although there had been no significant emergencies on campus in quite some time, you never know what could happen. They decided to gather data, visit other campuses, and create a crisis intervention plan to be prepared in the event that an emergency were to occur at Litchfield. Principal Maggie Wall facilitated the research, planning, implementation, and piloting of the plan. A strategic team with representatives from faculty, students, parents, and community members was selected to coordinate the efforts within the learning community.

During their research, the team learned there was no lock-down procedure in place for impending violence or other crises. There were also no communication measures beyond the use of the public address system. The team collected data from various sources and visited several schools, brainstorming potential ideas that would meet the needs of Litchfield High. Based on their research, they decided to implement a two-way radio system to facilitate communication between all faculty and staff. Different scenarios were posed in question-and-answer sessions with students, parents, the police department, and other community agencies. Precise procedures were developed, articulated, and practiced in a similar manner to fire and weather drills. Based on the results of their research, planning, and practice sessions, the learning community felt they developed and implemented a good crisis management plan that is unique to the needs of their school.

Reflective Analysis: Pause and Think

1. Develop a crisis management plan that would be effective for your school. Use research-based data collection methods and community agencies.

2. Compare and contrast safety and security procedures at your school with those of a generation ago. In what ways, if any, have they changed? How could they be improved?

3. If things have changed, what societal factors have contributed to these changes?

4. Describe proactive things that school stakeholders can do to decrease the likelihood that they will need to implement a crisis intervention plan.

5. Describe specific ways the school community can be involved in the development of a crisis intervention plan. How can they become engaged in both the process and the product?

6. Create a scenario involving a perceived crisis and a proactive reaction.

7. How can the school community be engaged in collaborative planning to meet the changing operational needs of a campus?

Resources: Aligned Budget Development

Caroline Meeker, principal of Thomas Edison Middle School, is concerned about the equity of resource allocation for her growing population of bilingual students. During the last 2 years, Edison has experienced a 14% increase in new students from a specific region of Nicaragua. With the assistance of the campus budget committee, she analyzes current expenditures against student needs and finds significant differences. To this end, the instructional strategies committee has recommended hiring an additional bilingual teacher midyear to work with students with limited English proficiency before standardized testing begins.

The budget committee agrees that there is inequity in resource allocation with campus needs and goals. They recommend that modifications should be made as quickly as possible. After considerable discussion, the budget committee recommends the transferring of funds from other campus projects to hiring the additional bilingual teacher. During this time, Mrs. Meeker works closely with several community groups to supplement funds the campus hopes to reallocate.

Stakeholders at Edison agree to the proposed changes endorsed by the budget committee, and a new teacher is hired. Unfortunately, the teacher is absent almost as often as she is present and ultimately must be removed from her position. Although various substitute teachers are used during her absence, they are not invested in the success of the program, students, or campus. Teachers and others at Edison are concerned that the lack of consistency in the tutorial program implementation will adversely affect the results they had hoped to achieve. They are afraid that if scores for the new students do not improve, adequate funding will not be allocated for next year when they hope to have a committed teacher who attends school regularly and is invested in the success of Edison and its students.

Reflective Analysis: Pause and Think

1. Describe additional ways resources could be collaboratively obtained from diverse community sources to fund the new program the students at Edison need.

2. Describe the ideal relationship of faculty, staff, and other learning community members with administrators in the budget development process.

3. Develop and explain ways the principal should utilize parents and other community members in the design of the campus budget.

4. As an educational leader, describe types of data necessary to analyze in guiding decision making for internal and external funding, budget development, and expenditures.

5. The local chapter of the League of Latin American Citizens (LULAC) has donated a sizeable sum of money to be used for supplemental resources or programming to assist students at your school who speak limited English or who are new immigrants to the United States. Design a model for fund use that incorporates the academic, physical, and emotional needs of students acclimating to a new culture. Identify, describe, and incorporate resources other than money from the LULAC chapter.

6. Describe the role of external funding to support student success. In what ways could potential sources be identified and funding procured?

7. Identify and analyze the roles and responsibilities of school community stakeholders in the soliciting, obtaining, and managing external funds.

ACTIVITIES FOR PROFESSIONAL DEVELOPMENT

The principal should

- Initiate action research and evaluation projects necessary to the effective organization and operation of schools
- Develop training for the learning community on organizational health and development, budget planning, and alignment of resources with campus goals
- Coordinate campus needs assessments to align with campus goals and priorities
- Lead planning to increase the diversity of school organizational techniques and personnel
- Facilitate the development of a campus crisis intervention plan
- Coordinate activities on crisis intervention in conjunction with local agencies
- Host a school forum with diverse community agencies and representatives to discuss collaborative partnerships to enhance safe schools
- Stage mock emergency drills and evaluate their effectiveness, making and implementing recommendations for modifications as needed
- Facilitate teambuilding and conflict-resolution strategies stressing mutual respect between all stakeholders with students, faculty, and other members of the learning community
- Provide opportunities for faculty, staff, and themselves to attend professional conferences designed to keep abreast of new developments, trends, and issues affecting students as well as potential strategies to address them

- Sponsor a celebration dinner at the end of each year in recognition of the contributions of all members of the organization working together for the safe, efficient, and effective operation of the school and highlighting specific successes that have occurred

CONCLUSIONS

In summary, educational leaders must promote the success of all students by ensuring management of the organization, operations, and resources necessary for a safe, efficient, and effective learning environment. These goals are accomplished in a myriad of ways, but the purpose remains consistent. Without a safe, efficient, and effective learning environment, teachers will not be able to teach to the best of their ability, and students will not be able to learn to the best of their abilities.

These concepts are simple. Implementation is not. Principals must be on constant alert at all times, proactively soliciting funds, communicating, and leading in an ethical and equitable manner to enhance every facet of student growth and opportunity. Creating a balance between being a visionary and manager is a difficult task as the principal seeks to wear multiple hats at the same time. That is the integrated nature of the job and a definition of the principalship. We are the ones primarily responsible for the safe, efficient, and effective organization and operation of the school. The buck stops here.

The Ultimate Application

1. Develop a model to be used by the school community on how to determine and prioritize campus needs, which will be used in vision, goals, budget, and staff development.

2. Identify and analyze factors that contribute to low and high faculty and staff morale.

3. Describe the relationship between faculty morale and organizational efficiency and productivity.

4. Evaluate and make recommendations concerning procedures and policies used in your school for the equitable selection of new employees.

5. Describe the learning environment at your school. Explain the role of the community in facilitating a safe, efficient, and effective learning environments.

6. Describe a plan whereby families and schools work together to enhance the organizational oversight of the school.

7. Describe a budget development process that uses the learning community and is aligned with the campus vision and goals.

CHAPTER SIX

Together We Build
The Strength of Collaborative Partnerships

STANDARD 4:

A school administrator is an educational leader who promotes the success of all students by collaborating with families and community members, responding to diverse community interests and needs, and mobilizing community resources.

The old saying "no man is an island" means that no one lives in isolation. The same is true for schools. No longer can schools operate simply within the confines of their own facilities. Schools and communities must work together in collaborative partnerships for the benefit of society as a whole. Our schools are integral parts of the community. It is up to us to be leaders in reaching out to other entities to develop collaborative partnerships for the benefit of students and families. Similar to the teamwork spirit to be developed inside the school through culture, climate, and vision, we as educators are the arm that must take leadership in reaching out to the community to create that same "together we can" spirit.

PHILOSOPHICAL FRAMEWORK

Collaboration

As we reach out to divergent groups and issues within our communities, one of the first things we must do is learn to "seek first to understand" other people's interests, needs, and perspectives (Covey, 1990b). This is essential in developing effective communication and relationships with families and other community members, groups, and agencies. It is also the backbone to the development of collaborative partnerships. People are not always going to agree with each other. Different groups address issues from divergent perspectives due to various factors such as race, gender, religion, culture, and politics. As long as each group is determined to hold onto its own perspectives without thinking about how the other group feels, it will be difficult to develop respectful collaborative relationships. In a healthy exchange of ideas, it is inevitable that conflict will arise. The principal as facilitator must give voice to all stakeholders, identify common values, and resolve conflict while building the team, its unity, and its vision. When each group is willing to stop, reflect, and think about where the other group is coming from, progress can be made. This does not mean either group has to give up its convictions. It does mean that true communication instead of rhetoric can begin to occur. While not giving in to the other opinion, each side gains perspective of where the other is coming from. Once that occurs, common ground can be established, and people can begin laying a foundation for conflict resolution and problem solving. In seeking to develop collaborative partnerships with groups internal and external to the school, the principal must be knowledgeable about the issues and trends that affect families and community members. First steps in this process are to "seek first to understand" different perspectives, facilitate open yet respectful discussion, and identify common values to use as starting points.

Families are critical in this process. After all, without families we would not have students. Families and their children are our first priority. We must solicit and welcome them, encourage them to become an integral part of our school community; use their talents and skills, particularly in the areas of appreciating and responding to diversity; and recognize that they usually have the best interests of their children in their hearts, just as we do. This interest must be appreciated, valued, and acknowledged. Families are critical stakeholders in the learning community and therefore valuable assets. Students of all ages need the physical and effective support of their families and schools to face and respond to the challenges of society. With the changing times, it is even more critical that schools, families, and all other stakeholders work together in collaborative partnerships that focus on the needs of children. The more we involve others in informed, data-driven decision making, the better. It provides ownership in the process, the product, and the school itself. All of these are good things for students as well as communities as a whole. It requires effort to develop mutually trusting relationships, especially with families whose views may be radically different from the mainstream of the school. We work hard to include everyone, even those who are reluctant to take part, and we keep trying, being persistent in overcoming barriers to success. We never give up on anyone or anything. We keep nurturing, soliciting, and valuing whatever tidbits of cooperation we can get. Then we build on our small successes and lay a strong foundation of communication, cooperation, and collaboration for the future.

Dealing with the public means that educational leaders must have refined public relations skills. We must know how to be polite and diplomatic even when we are secretly biting our tongues. There will be many times when what we *want* to say is not what we *can* say. Even when we do manage to say the right thing, there's still a good chance we'll be misperceived or quoted incorrectly. To address this problem, most districts have a full-time public relations staff to handle official news releases, impromptu media calls, and crisis situations, cases in which it is vital to have a good relationship with the media. During times of crisis, members of the media can be your best friends or your worst enemies. During the best of times, you need them to present a positive imagine of your school to the public. Remember never to pick a fight with anyone who buys ink by the barrel. Not only will you rarely win, there is little to be gained from a media battle. Instead, invite the press to good things that are happening at your school. Solicit their involvement. Provide them with information about positive, creative, and unusual things that are happening. We need to do a better job of marketing our schools and our vision of excellence. Soliciting collaborative relationships with the media is a big step in that direction. We need all the good press we can get. You can bet that when something bad happens, the media will find out and publicize it. To combat this, we must be proactive, inviting and involving them in as many good things as possible. They may not come, but always solicit their involvement and make them feel welcome. Let them experience your climate and culture. Use their marketing abilities to articulate the vision and passion that makes your school unique and successful, a vibrant place for students to learn.

There are all sorts of community agencies with services designed to help families meet the demands of life. Actually, public school systems are among them. It is our role to improve society by producing literate, self-supporting citizens who make a contribution to their world. This gives us a common purpose that we share with various service agencies. Civic clubs, churches, service organizations, businesses, social service agencies, and institutions of higher education are all prime targets to develop alliances with and create "win–win" (Covey, 1990b) partnerships. Most of them have opportunities or resources for outreach. Many schools have developed creative partnerships with unique community groups (such as a "Tennis Shoe Fund," "Coat Fund," or "Story Book Fund") by thinking outside the box to help students have what they need to succeed or simply to have a better existence.

Be visible. Be proactive. Leave the school. Go visiting. Tell your school's story, its triumphs, and its needs. Solicit help, input, alliances, and partnerships. But do not just go with your hand out. Ask what the school can do for them in return. Most of these groups will want nothing, but you should ask anyway. Send notes of appreciation with specific feedback and examples of how contributions, service, or resources have helped an individual student, a class, a grade, or the school. These kinds of personal narratives in which people can see their efforts have had a direct impact on the life of students will bear various fruitful returns in the future.

Remember, we are the schools of the United States of America. As a country, we have an inbred respect for education, a concern for our young, and a pragmatic attitude of doing what it takes to get things done to create a better tomorrow. All our tomorrows are directly linked to our children. As a collaborative school team, we should plan ways to solicit and involve multiple stakeholders from families and the entire community to become involved and invested in the progress of our schools toward our collaboratively developed vision of excellence. What others may not be able to supply in money, they may be able to supply in time, talents, expertise, or other resources. But the number-one thing we need to solicit actively and positively every day is support. We need the support of the entire school community. It does not happen overnight or by chance. It happens by getting out of our offices and into the community, being visible, proactive, and vocal about the successes and the needs of individual students and our schools. We take what we can get, whatever that is, and sincerely thank our benefactors. Then we invite them to school to see what a wonderful, enticing place we have where teachers teach, students learn, and all of us together are actively engaged in creating a better tomorrow.

Community Interest and Needs

Every community has its own special interests and needs. Different things have different values in different places. This does not make one place or value right and another wrong. It just means they are different. It is the role of the schools to research and discern both the interests and the needs of the communities that they serve. A major way to do this is to become actively involved and visible in community activities and organizations. Like it or not, you are a living, breathing representative and voice for the school system— and particularly for your campus. When people in the community see you, they see your school. Everything you say or do reflects back on the school you represent. Remember that. This can be serious business, particularly in smaller communities where schools and educators are often under close scrutiny.

You will need to use appropriate assessment strategies and research methods to discern what the needs and interests of the community are so you and your school can address them. It is not something you can do once and then check off your "To Do" list. Communities are ever changing, so their needs and interests change, too. Things that seem vital at one point in time will shift from importance as something else takes their place. Schools must be vigilantly cognizant of these changes, staying on top of current issues and themes and developing proactive measures to address them collaboratively with the community. This is particularly true in the area of changing demographics and increasing diversity of culture through ethnicity, race, religion, culture, or any type of special interest group. You can never ignore community interests and needs. Stay actively involved, keeping your thumb on the pulse of the community, knowing its priorities and how the school fits into that picture. Schools are a microsystem of society. The diversity, culture, and values of a community are reflected in its schools. You must use assessment strategies, research methods, and common sense to address the conditions and dynamics of your individual school community. You must seek collaborative partnerships with all entities to help all stakeholders improve society and to enhance teaching and learning as something of vital importance for our future.

One way to do that is to capitalize on diversity within the community. Solicit input from multiple stakeholders from different external entities. Remember that diversity involves more than race, gender, culture, and religion. It can mean socioeconomic status, political preference, and special interests; it can mean differing learning modalities and disabilities; it can mean having exceptional needs. People from diverse groups are part of our learning communities, and they are part of society. We should reach out to all of them and bring them into the school as valued assets. Solicit support, input, and resources for them. In a partnership, each group gives, receives, and benefits. Collectively as a school, think about what you have to give and about what benefits you could receive. Schools, too, are a service entity. We need to hold up our end of partnerships by giving to as well as receiving from all stakeholders.

Community Resources

Standard 2 addressed the appropriate and efficient use of school resources in general. Now we talk specifically about the appropriate and effective use of *public* resources. Part of being a good steward of the vision is to be a good steward of all resources—and of taxpayer dollars—to ensure the prudent use of resources to solve problems or to promote student achievement. It also includes using resources that help the school achieve its goals. After all, everything we do and everything we use should be focused on achieving a school goal that, of course, must ultimately support the vision of excellence. Everything we do must focus on promoting the success of all students. Don't waste time or resources on anything that does not fit into this category.

Likewise, we can do our part to support community and social service agencies. Remember, a partnership is not a one-way street. Think of it as a seesaw delicately balanced between each stakeholder. There will be times when various outside agencies will need and solicit our help. As good stewards of the vision, we must do everything possible to reciprocate when members of the community come to us in need. Of course, we must remember that everything we do—particularly if it involves money or other resources—must be legal and in accordance with policy. So many potential problems can be averted by checking ahead of time to ensure that a plan is legal, ethical, and within regulatory guidelines. Bearing this in mind, share resources and multiply effort, rewards, and results by working with others. In so doing, schools become good neighbors and collaborative partners, strengthening relationships between the school and community.

Following are three case studies that address the issues of collaboration, community interest and needs, and community resources. Read, pause, reflect, and think what you would do if you were the educational leader of these schools.

CASE STUDIES

Collaboration: Collaborative Partnerships With Higher Education

As principal of Paul Meyer High School, Francis Cooke was interested in developing a collaborative partnership with an institution of higher education. The students of Meyer High School are primarily from low socioeconomic households. A small percentage of students attend college after high school graduation. Francis feels that if he could work out a partnership with a local college, it would benefit his students. Although he had not worked out the specifics of his idea, he did contact a midsized university within 20 miles of Meyer High. He contacted the director of program development to explain his formative idea. The two decided to meet to discuss it further.

The next week, they met for lunch and agreed that Francis's plan could be mutually beneficial for both the school and the university. The high school students could gain from having regular exposure to college students in various capacities. For example, college students could sponsor intramural activities, tutor individuals and groups, speak at assembly programs, and serve as mentors to at-risk young people. The university would also benefit if more Meyer High graduates applied for admission to the university in subsequent years. Both educators were excited about the possibilities of this collaborative partnership. They agreed to meet again to further develop their ideas and to solicit others to facilitate implementation of the program.

Regretfully, the project languished and never got off the ground. Upon reflection, Francis realized there were several reasons this had occurred. Both administrators were so busy that neither had the time to fully develop or implement the project. Another problem was that they had not defined timelines, responsibilities, and expectations. The two educators also were unable to integrate sufficient stakeholders to make the plan work. Talking on the phone at a later date, Francis and the university administrator agreed they would try again sometime in the future.

Reflective Analysis: Pause and Think

1. Although both leaders agreed that Francis's plan could be mutually beneficial, the project never got off the ground. For one thing, there was a lack of empowerment of and delegation to others in the process, as well as insufficient development of the idea. Explain the importance of empowerment and delegation in organizational leadership.

2. Describe ways Francis could have empowered and involved others in the idea of a high school–university collaborative.

3. Could this potential partnership be salvaged? If so, what would it take?

4. Develop a model of collaboration that could be mutually beneficial for a school with an institution of higher education.

5. Describe factors that should be involved in a school–university partnership.

6. Develop a flow chart including goals, strategies, delegated responsibilities, a timeline for implementation, and an evaluative process for a potential collaborative partnership between a school and an external agency, group, or club.

Community Interest and Needs: Uniforms and Sexual Abstinence

For the last several years, Mary J. Collins Middle School has instituted a series of monthly open discussion meetings. The purpose of these meetings is to provide a forum for parents and other community members to ask questions and discuss trends and issues that affect the school and community. Principal Dade Zarrabi has found the top two topics of discussion this year to be particularly interesting, drawing good-sized audiences to the meetings. The topics are whether Collins should implement a policy requiring students, faculty, and staff to wear uniforms starting with the next school year and whether the school should implement a sexual abstinence program within the confines of the physical education classes.

Proponents of the uniform policy say that uniforms would be less expensive than regular clothing, would cut down on peer pressure for name-brand clothing, would reduce disciplinary referrals, and would raise test scores. Opponents say uniforms are too expensive, would be problematic for students that enter the school after the year has begun, and stifle individual student expression and creativity. Proponents for the sexual abstinence program point to the large number of teen pregnancies and sexually transmitted diseases as reasons the program is needed. Opponents say it is the family's responsibility, not the school's, to discuss these issues with their children.

Needless to say, these open discussions have been lively. Principal Zarrabi and the faculty talked about the open discussions at a recent faculty meeting. Some members of the faculty felt the discussions were too "lively" and might get out of hand in the future if they were not handled properly. Others felt it was important to provide a forum where teachers, parents, and community members could discuss issues openly, pointing out that as yet no meetings had gotten out of control.

Reflective Analysis: Pause and Think

1. Are open forum discussions a good or bad idea? Support your response.

2. What group process safeguards should be incorporated into the meetings to keep them from getting out of control? In what type of models should the principal be trained and prepared for meeting facilitation and control?

3. How should input from the forums be used?

4. What criteria, if any, should be used to determine if a topic is suitable or appropriate for an open forum discussion?

5. Should the principal serve as the moderator of these forums, or would another community member with specific training on the topic under discussion be a better choice? Support your response.

6. What positive and negative outcomes could potentially come from these forums?

7. Would discussions such as these be better suited for smaller group discussions? If so, describe the format.

Community Resources: Capitalizing on Diversity

Elizabeth Siegler is principal of Louisa May Alcott Elementary School. During the last decade, the student population has changed from primarily white to about 65% minority. The largest growth has occurred among African American students. Ms. Siegler and a committee of learning community members are interviewing candidates for the vice principalship. They are cognizant that the person they select must be able to work well within the changing demographics and culture of the school.

They are delighted with the credentials of Noel Cameron, a young African American man with a passion for students and community outreach. One of the things Noel stressed in his interview was his strong desire to work in the community as a representative of the school. The team selected Noel for the job.

Noel wasted no time getting busy. He moved into the community, joined a local church, and became involved in several other community organizations. He had an engaging, outgoing personality that he used as a proactive spokesman for the school and as an advocate for the needs of students on every possible occasion. He actively made home visits, encouraging volunteerism and participation in the school community, particularly among other African American families. He set up a tutorial program with students from a local junior college and solicited additional tutors from his church and elsewhere. He worked to develop a Big Brother, Big Sister program targeting minority students, yet he showed no partiality and mentored all students. Noel was a tremendous asset to the vision, culture, and climate of Alcott Elementary, and he became a voice of activism and support for the school, its students, and their families.

Reflective Analysis: Pause and Think

1. Why is it important for people other than the principal to be involved in the selection of new faculty and staff members and new administrators?

2. Should cultural sensitivity be a criteria in job applicant selection? Why or why not?

3. Identify the characteristics of Noel's outreach endeavors and demeanor that made him an asset to Alcott Elementary and its learning community.

4. Describe the benefits of these traits for the students, the school, and the community.

5. What additional things could Noel and other educational leaders do to reach out to diverse community resources and families?

6. Using data for appropriate decision making, define and describe specific areas at your school that would most benefit from a volunteer program.

ACTIVITIES FOR PROFESSIONAL DEVELOPMENT

The principal should

- Know, be known, and be actively involved in the school community
- Build connections with diverse community stakeholders for the benefit of the school and community
- Be actively involved in many community organizations and functions and encourage all members of the learning community, including students, to also be active participants
- Initiate ongoing discussions with families, businesses, and other community members on the continuing and expanding vision of the school and its place in a democratic society
- Facilitate training in acknowledging, responding to, and appreciating diversity in the school and the larger community
- Implement conversational foreign language classes aligned with community needs for members of the faculty and staff and implement English classes for parents and other community members
- Lead ongoing discussions within the school and community on the importance of an inclusive learning environment
- With parents, teachers, and other school community members, brainstorm ways to create a campus culture and climate that would welcome and nurture students, families, and other community members from diverse backgrounds
- Initiate opportunities for the school community to develop partnerships with external social, educational, cultural, and business agencies to fulfill the mission of success for all young people

- Devise a plan to quantitatively and qualitatively identify students who would benefit most from a volunteer tutorial program and monitor their progress
- Work with teachers and parents to develop a tutoring program that could subsequently be implemented and monitored as a trained parental volunteer project
- Accompany and empower others to proactively solicit needed and supplemental community resources necessary to the success of students
- Provide professional consultants to train administrators and faculty and staff members on grant writing and procurement to meet campus needs
- Never take no for an answer when seeking to do what is best for students and their families

CONCLUSIONS

In summary, to create effective and collaborative partnerships between schools and communities, educational leaders must research and synthesize the specific and changing interests, needs, issues, and trends of the community to respond appropriately and effectively. We must reach out to multiple stakeholders, including families, social service agencies, and the media, to create collaborative partnerships in which everyone gives and receives. We must be good stewards of public resources of every description and good neighbors to the communities in which we are a microsystem. We must be highly involved and visible within community organizations, activities, and functions because, whether we like it or not, we are the face and voice of the school. We must make diversity our friend, soliciting input from multiple and conflicting perspectives, seeking first to understand other points of view rather than criticizing or dismissing them. This is particularly important when dealing with issues involving students with disabilities, handicaps, or different learning modalities, as well as those of various races, religions, and cultures. The idea is to create a common bond of understanding in which everything we say or do is aimed at enhancing teaching and learning. We want our students to be equipped to solve problems and achieve their goals. To do this, we must work to develop collaborative relationships with families and external agencies to promote success for all. In so doing, individual needs can be met, increased learning will be facilitated, and the future of our democratic society will be enriched.

The Ultimate Application

1. Describe the implications of community partnerships and support for your school.

2. Describe the role of the principal, faculty, and staff in developing collaborative partnerships with external groups and agencies.

3. Describe the effects of community partnerships on student achievement. How could they be researched and enhanced?

4. The importance of diversity in society is well documented. Describe the benefits of a diversified school environment and its relationship to the school community.

5. Compare and contrast the pros and cons of having volunteers in schools, including legal perspectives. Draw conclusions.

6. Describe steps that should be taken to enhance a school's poor community image.

7. Discuss ways to encourage parents to become an integral part of the school, even if they do not speak English fluently.

8. Describe steps schools can take to generate community support in rural, suburban, and urban settings. Are there differences in the appropriate contextual steps? If so, describe them.

CHAPTER SEVEN

Taking a Stand
The Moral Dilemma

STANDARD 5:

A school administrator is an educational leader who promotes the success of all students by acting with integrity, fairness, and in an ethical manner.

Standard 5 sums up all the other standards. If we are appropriately and prudently researching, analyzing, synthesizing, soliciting, advocating, nurturing, and sustaining everything that relates to school leadership, then we are doing those things. In so doing, we would be promoting the success of all students by acting with integrity, fairness, and in an ethical manner. The problem is that not everyone is doing everything they should, which explains why we need Standard 5.

Many states and professional organizations have developed their own codes of conduct and ethical practice for educators. The code of conduct for the state of Texas has been used as a model in the quest for educator integrity, fairness, and ethical behavior. It is available online from the Texas State Board for Educator Certification at *http://www.sbec.state.tx.us/*. Click on Code of Ethics.

PHILOSOPHICAL FRAMEWORK

Integrity

All school leaders must act with integrity. When we lose our integrity, we lose our effectiveness. People will no longer trust us. Trust is an easy thing to lose and an incredibly difficult thing to regain. It is difficult and time-consuming to rebuild trust in a relationship with someone who has hurt you. Students, faculty, staff, and the community must be able to trust you, to know that even if you make an unpopular decision, you did so based on facts rather than favoritism. They need to know that you do not have any ulterior motives, that you are honest, and that the best interests of the school and community are of utmost importance to you. Act consistently and treat all people equitably. Show stakeholders in the school and the community that you genuinely care about them. Nurture, sustain, and advocate for every person and for the school vision. Demonstrate respect for every stakeholder through honesty; hold confidences and treat everyone with dignity regardless of his or her circumstances. In these ways, the community will see you as the steward of the vision, as deserving of trust. In other words, they will see you as a person of integrity.

In short, stakeholders need to know that you are a principal with character, that you value honor, and that you are driven by an unending passion to do everything you can to promote the success of all students, faculty and staff members, families—of the entire learning community—to reach a vision of excellence.

Fairness

You cannot play favorites. Sometimes difficult decisions must be made that involve people, products, or programs. You may have strong feelings about something and a natural tendency to lean one way or the other in your decision making. This is called bias—the archenemy of assessment and evaluation. Sometimes even the best leaders can be unintentionally biased. You must build safeguards into your decision-making process to check yourself, to provide consistency, and to ensure equity and fairness.

It is not a bad thing to admit that you've made a mistake. In fact, it is far better to have the courage to admit you were wrong than to follow a dead horse down a dead-end road or to keep beating your head against a wall that isn't budging. Analyze and learn from your mistake. Handle the situation in a strong yet humble manner, admit that you made a mistake, articulate how you plan to correct it, apologize if you hurt anyone, then focus on the future and how you all, collectively, will do better next time. This proves you are human, and humans make mistakes. If you have been a standards-based leader, you will have been forgiving, nurturing, and insightful in helping members of the school community reflect on their own errors. You will have modeled stewardship of the vision by helping others when they have made mistakes. Now they can return the favor. Admitting a mistake does not mean you are weak or inept. It proves that you are human, that you see where you went wrong, that you'll correct it, and that you'll learn from your experience.

If you want to be treated fairly, you must treat others fairly. You must demonstrate impartiality to students, teachers, and families, be sensitive and equitable to all forms of diversity, exhibit ethical behavior at all times, and expect the same from others. If you do these things, you will be a leader who deserves respect, not simply because of your position, but because you have earned it. Likewise, set the same expectations for students and everyone else in the learning community. Be equitable and fair to everyone. Your behavior will speak for itself and reap multiple benefits for the culture, climate, and equity of the campus.

Ethics

Principals must be ethical and above board in every aspect of their lives. All decisions must be based on good judgment and basic moral and ethical standards; they must also fall within legal and policy guidelines. This sounds obvious. But some ethical decisions are not so simple. You may see two sides of an issue, and each may have its pros and cons. In these instances, what you are supposed to do?

There are no easy answers to ethical questions. In all cases, you must seriously consider every aspect of the situation, empower those involved in the decision-making process, stay open-minded, analyze all factors, and then reach the best data-driven conclusion you can based on the information presented. No one ever said being a school leader was easy. Thankfully, you won't face the really difficult decisions every day. But you will face them. Expect them, and be prepared. Then do your best to resolve them with integrity and fairness.

The Rotary Club International has something they call the Four Way Test, comprising four questions Rotarians should ask themselves when confronting any issue. They are as follows:

1. Is it the truth?

2. Is it fair to all concerned?

3. Will it build goodwill and better friendships?

4. Will it be beneficial to all concerned?

If you think about it, the Rotarians are on to a good thing. What if, with the permission of the Rotarians, we kept questions 1, 2, and 4, but modified the third one: Will it build goodwill and facilitate greater student learning and success? Wow! Those four simple questions would then comprise as good a set of educators' ethical benchmarks as I've seen anywhere. Why not put them to work?

Following are three case studies of situations in which principals addressed the issues of integrity, fairness, and ethics. Analyze them and think about what you would do in similar circumstances.

CASE STUDIES

Integrity: Respect for All Stakeholders

Central Elementary School, located in a suburban district, is known for having a warm, supportive climate and culture that supports all members of the school community. There is a collegial and respectful attitude among faculty, staff, administration, families, and students. Parents are supportive of campus goals and participate actively in multiple volunteer opportunities. Central is considered a popular and successful environment for teachers to teach and students to learn.

Mrs. Beardley is a fourth-grade teacher at Central. She is the only employee about whom the principal, Annabella Sokolewicz, receives consistent complaints from parents, other teachers, and students themselves. Although Mrs. Beardley is successful in instructional matters, she promotes a poor, nonsupportive learning environment in the classroom. She makes snide remarks to students, and when confronted, she claims to have been misquoted or that things were taken out of context, acknowledges the remark but says it was followed by something else that was nicer, or denies that she said anything at all. Even though classes are heterogeneously grouped, she always claims to have the worst students academically and behaviorally. The classroom environment resembles boot camp rather than a place where students are actively engaged in hands-on, constructive learning. Mrs. Beardley rarely participates in campus extracurricular activities or faculty parties, claiming she does not feel well. She plans ahead to be absent for student fieldtrips, assemblies, PTA-sponsored programs, or any activity that will occur outdoors. She displays no respect for students, a nurturing climate and culture, or any campus traditions and rituals. Because she always has an excuse for anything with which she is confronted, Ms. Sokolewicz is perplexed as to what to do to get Mrs. Beardley to respond respectfully and appropriately to students and the Central vision.

Reflective Analysis: Pause and Think

1. In what ways should Ms. Sokolewicz address this situation with Mrs. Beardley?

2. Develop a professional growth plan for Mrs. Beardley that will focus on targeted goals related to respect, integrity, and providing a nurturing learning environment for her students.

3. When parents complain about Mrs. Beardley to Ms. Sokolewicz and she knows they are right but have no substantive evidence, how should she handle her responses?

4. Mrs. Beardley approaches the principal to tell her she will be absent on Career Day because she has an appointment with her doctor. Ms. Sokolewicz has no doubt this is true because the teacher always schedules something so she will be absent on nontraditional school days. In what way should the principal handle this situation?

5. Mrs. Beardley never comes to faculty luncheons or after-school gatherings sponsored by the PTA or other school groups. Her regular absences reinforce a perception within the school community that she is not an integral part of the school culture of warmth and collegiality. In what ways could other stakeholders encourage her to attend and to show support for the sponsoring organizations as well as the school vision?

6. After repeated informal discussions about her attitude, in a summative conference Ms. Sokolewicz formally addressed these issues with Mrs. Beardley. Mrs. Beardley did not deny any of Ms. Sokolewicz's points, but rather said that people just did not like her and that she did not feel well. What should Ms. Sokolewicz do?

7. With a partner, participate in nonscripted role-playing in which each of you have the opportunity to practice being the principal and teacher. Role play a conference between the two in which the principal tries to help the teacher see that she is displaying a disrespectful, passive–aggressive attitude, while the teacher counters defensively. Reverse roles so each can practice the other position. In each case, stay with it until the situation is resolved in a positive manner.

Fairness: Oh, Those Cheerleaders!

Cheerleader selection is often a tedious and emotional experience for school administrators. During the weeks before tryouts at Ridgewood Middle School, the faculty sponsors, Ms. Funkhouser and Ms. Leffingwell, worked closely with the campus team and with the principal, Mrs. Bailey, to review the rules and guidelines for participation and selection. In turn, Ms. Funkhouser and Ms. Leffingwell went over the rules orally. Then they provided each girl a written list of the rules and required each girl and one of her parents to sign a statement that they had read and understood the rules. Each girl and her parents did so.

One rule stated that all candidates must attend school on the day of tryouts, but one candidate was absent that day. Rumors circulated among the other girls that Cindy had said she was going to be absent that day to get her hair and nails done. Mrs. Bailey heard the rumors but doubted they were true. She checked with the sponsors to see if Cindy and either of her parents had signed the rules. She was shown the signature pages to verify that they had read and understood the rules. She also alerted the office staff to notify her if Cindy were to return to campus during the day.

During last period, Cindy showed up for school. When she appeared in the office, the staff notified Mrs. Bailey. She talked to Cindy to see where she had been during the day. Cindy said her grandfather had died, and that she had attended the funeral. Mrs. Bailey expressed her condolences and asked her grandfather's name, which Cindy slowly supplied. Interestingly, Mrs. Bailey's secretary had attended the funeral of that gentleman earlier that morning. She excused herself and talked with her secretary, who said that she had no idea he was Cindy's grandfather and that no, she had not seen Cindy at the funeral.

When Mrs. Bailey confronted Cindy, she acknowledged that the man was not her grandfather, and that she had not attended the funeral. After extended conversation, she admitted that she had lied, that she did have her hair and nails done, and that she had gone shopping with her older sister to buy a new outfit to wear to tryouts that afternoon. In fact, she produced a sales ticket with that day's date. Mrs. Bailey reminded Cindy that she had broken the rules and told her she would not be allowed to try out. Cindy became hysterical. She was allowed to call her mother, who was also upset because she had no idea that Cindy wasn't at school. Nonetheless, she felt this was a family problem and that Cindy should be allowed to try out. After all, Cindy had told her that she was better than all the other candidates, so she was sure to be selected.

Reflective Analysis: Pause and Think

1. Should Cindy be allowed to try out? Justify your response.

2. Would it be fair to the other girls if Cindy were allowed to try out? Why or why not?

3. What ethical considerations should be assessed in this situation?

4. How should Mrs. Bailey respond when Cindy's mother claimed this was a family problem?

5. Prepare a set of potential rules and guidelines for the cheerleader selection process that would seek to proactively address potential problems that could arise.

6. The rest of the cheerleading candidates were nervous about their own tryouts and actively watched to see how Mrs. Bailey would handle Cindy's situation. How should this be handled? What, if anything, should the girls be told? What lessons should be learned?

7. In addition to whether Cindy should be allowed to try out, she lied to her principal about her whereabouts earlier that day. In what manner should this be addressed?

Ethics: Hidden Agendas

A position in the social studies department at William Travis High School was available. Camille Nelson, a social studies teacher in a nearby district, heard about the job and decided to apply. She had taught various subjects in social studies for 7 years. Her credentials and references were excellent. In fact, her peers elected her Teacher of the Year last year. She lived in the same district where Travis High School was located and had looked forward to an opening so she could work in the district where her children attend school. After her application, she heard several favorable comments from other teachers at Travis who were happy she had applied and who looked forward to working with her.

As time went by and Camille heard nothing official from administrators, she called the district human resources office to inquire about the status of the position. She was told the position had been filled. Camille heard from other teachers that the job had been given to a noncertified, first-year teacher who would assist with coaching responsibilities after school. She was very disappointed. Camille felt her experience and credentials had not been considered in the selection process, particularly because she did not even get the chance to interview for the position.

Reflective Analysis: Pause and Think

1. What was the role of the principal in this situation?

2. Was Camille treated in an ethical manner?

3. Should the need for support for extracurricular activities count more than credentials and experience in a job selection process?

4. What should Camille do about the situation? Should she apply for future positions at William Travis?

5. Describe a potential "win–win" situation for this scenario.

6. Analyze the federal laws in relation to discriminatory practices in personnel selection. Was what happened to Camille discriminatory or unethical? Support your response.

7. Address the issue of Affirmative Action with regard to the equitable selection of employees. What avenues are and are not legal in the selection process?

ACTIVITIES FOR PROFESSIONAL DEVELOPMENT

The principal should

- Lead discussions about the connections between integrity, fairness, and ethics and the necessity of a nurturing, supportive learning environment for students, faculty, and staff

- Initiate role-playing activities within faculty in which potential situations that create ethical dilemmas are played out with different players and solutions each time
- Initiate conflict resolution, diversity, and multicultural training that addresses moral issues in working with students, families, and communities
- Conduct frequent informal "walk-through" observations in classrooms, interacting with students and teachers for the dual purposes of showing support of ongoing work and also to create firsthand opportunities to see what is going on
- Individually and collectively support and recognize the good things that are observed through formal and informal classroom observations rather than focusing only on negative behaviors
- Provide training in individual goal-setting and professional development plans that incorporate principles of integrity, fairness, and ethics toward the school community
- Show support of proactive and creative endeavors by teachers and others that involve them beyond their job descriptions to facilitate student success in varied arenas
- Ask the counselor to collaboratively work with other child service specialists to develop a staff program on working with problem students in a positive manner without negative verbal and nonverbal confrontations
- Empower teachers with the opportunity to develop specific criteria for student behavior management with definitions of what constitutes inappropriate behavior, what the consequences will be, what generates the necessity for an office referral, and the importance of detail and accuracy in record keeping
- Facilitate the development of specific rules and criteria for the selection of all student-based auditions and elections
- Demonstrate integrity, fairness, and ethics in all situations
- Appreciate diversity and multicultural issues and respond to them from an ethical and moral perspective
- Facilitate the articulation of established rules and guidelines related to all student and teacher activities

- Provide training in legal and ethical parameters in the selection and employment of staff and faculty
- Provide seminars that explore ethical and legal behavior and facilitate reflective opportunities to grow in integrity and professionalism
- Purchase books and other resources on ethical and legal issues and make them available to all faculty and staff; facilitate discussion and application groups on their contents
- Encourage teachers to use resource materials on ethical and legal issues in class, providing students with opportunities for discussion, interaction, and role playing

CONCLUSIONS

In summary, being a school leader is not an easy job. In many ways, the moral and ethical decisions are the hardest ones we make. Naïve thinkers outside of education may think these would be easy, but they are wrong. Decisions are not always clearly defined. School leadership is a tough job and not for the faint of heart. You must have courage, valor, and strength to weather turmoil, conflict, and difficult choices. You must walk with confidence knowing that as long as you keep focused on what is best, fair, and consistent, you cannot get too far off base.

When you look in the mirror each day, sincerely ask yourself if you are leading a life of integrity and fairness and if you exhibit ethical, respectful behavior. If there is ever a day when your sincere response is "Well, I'm not sure about how I'm handling . . . ," it's time to take time off to reflect and rethink who you are; what you are doing; if your behavior is truly distinguished by integrity, fairness, ethics; and if your life is in congruence with your personal mission. Life can get so busy that it's easy for things to fall out of perspective before you realize it. The key is taking time to reflect and genuinely examine our behavior, our goals, our mission—and ourselves. Applying these steps on a regular basis will pull us back to our true priorities, make us better human beings, and guarantee that we are better school leaders.

The Ultimate Application

1. Reflect on and explain the importance of all educators displaying the highest standards of integrity, fairness, and ethics.

2. Describe a situation in which you felt an administrator acted in an unethical manner. How could the situation have been handled in a morally responsible way?

3. Describe a situation in which a teacher or paraprofessional acted in an unethical manner. How could this situation have been handled in a morally responsible way?

4. One teacher in a school gossips about students in the faculty workroom and other places. Although the principal has talked to him about it, the situation continues. Prescribe a plan for the teacher that centers on respect for students' rights to confidentiality and administrative professional and ethical behavior.

5. Prepare a generic set of guidelines that is fair and ethical for the selection of students for auditioned and elected positions.

6. Describe a potentially volatile situation in which a student is involved in a problem that needs an ethical and fair resolution. What should the principal do to resolve the situation appropriately?

CHAPTER EIGHT

Beware of the Alligators

The Politics of Administrative Leadership

STANDARD 6:

A school administrator is an educational leader who promotes the success of all students by understanding, responding to, and influencing the larger political, social, economic, legal, and cultural context.

S tandard 6 is an integrating, decisive factor in which various issues introduced in other standards are brought back to our attention. This time, the concepts of politics, social justice, economics, legal regulations, and cultural sensitivity are addressed from their larger contextual perspectives. They are studied as they relate to and shape both the school and the community. These issues may or may not occur directly inside the school but do have direct ramifications on students and families. Within this standard, the educational leader takes a proactive stand with representatives from diverse groups as an advocate for all children, regardless of socioeconomic background, race, ethnicity, gender, learning style, or any other differences.

PHILOSOPHICAL FRAMEWORK

Larger Context Knowledge

There is a distinction between knowledge and skills in Standard 6. Larger context knowledge relates to the myriad things of which educational leaders must have awareness and understanding, including political, social, economic, legal, and cultural theories and concepts. To do this, the principal must have knowledge and understanding of how the legal and political system works and the ramifications those systems have on shaping schools and communities. As overwhelming as that sounds, the application of those skills is equally challenging and somewhat daunting in magnitude. Furthermore, the principal must stay abreast of current and potential local, state, and federal law and policy development that also might have implications on students, families, or the school community. Going a step further, the principal must become an advocate for any factor that could improve educational and social opportunities and engage others to do likewise. In other words, educational leaders must become politically savvy on various levels and encourage those around them to do the same. There are many ways principals can do this. The important thing is to present a standard for the benefit of children and their families and to be a proactive voice and advocate for the needs of every child.

To be able to do these things, principals must be well read and cognizant of current events. They must be aware of and understand economic factors that shape the community because societal economics do have a direct impact on schools. If there is a bond or sales tax election—even if it is sponsored by different taxing entities, such as cities, counties, water districts, and so forth—there are still issues that will have direct or indirect impact on schools. It is your job to seek out what those impacts will be and proceed accordingly.

As with previous standards, the principal must understand, appreciate, and respond to all issues related to cultural diversity in the community and how these issues interact with the role of the school in promoting social justice. Social justice must be developed, nurtured, and sustained. As in Standards 4 and 5, the principal must understand the norms and values of the community to promote it.

The consequent effects on the learning community are vital to our being able to ascertain which issues or trends are relevant and can be used for school improvement. Just because something is not a direct issue on schools today does not mean that it will not become one tomorrow. Therefore, principals must be constantly vigilant to any changing mores and values and their possible impact on the school community. The necessity and effects of motivation and change theories as well as the conflict resolution skills introduced in Standards 1, 2, and 3, are reiterated here with consideration as to how they can actually be applied in the community. Whenever there is true dialogue and discourse, there will be some level of conflict. There is no such thing as a totally homogenous group. If there is not an open exchange of diverse thought, everyone sits around agreeing with each other, and this is a waste of valuable time that produces absolutely nothing. Without divergent opinions and perspectives, there can be no critical analysis. All discussions must be facilitated in a positive manner by persons skilled in group processes, change theories, interpersonal sensitivity, and conflict-resolution skills.

All of this boils down to having the appropriate knowledge to advocate for social justice for all segments of the community— particularly for children and families. It is impossible to advocate for these needs if you do not have the appropriate knowledge of political, social, economic, legal, and cultural issues.

State and federal legislatures consider issues that affect families every day. Policies and guidelines internal and external to the district can directly impact the lives of everyone within the learning community. How can you be actively involved, make knowledgeable decisions, and seek to engage others in advocacy if you do not know what is taking place in the larger societal context? Standard 6 says you should be knowledgeable about anything that affects teaching, learning, and families. But it goes beyond understanding these issues: You must respond to and influence the direction they take. To do this, you must stay well read, be involved within the larger community and state, and put yourself in positions to be cognizant of what is really going on in political, social, economic, legal, and cultural contexts. Being an educational leader is more encompassing than being an instructional leader. It encompasses all these other venues because they directly or indirectly affect teaching, learning, and the success of all students. Therefore, if you are not already involved in the larger community, get involved. All of this works together to make you the campus and community leader with the capability to do what needs to be done for students, families, and society.

Larger Context Skills

Having knowledge of the things we just discussed is one thing. Having the skills to use and apply them is something else entirely. Earlier we discussed the distinctions between being a great visionary and a great manager. Some administrators are skilled at one or the other, but what our schools need and deserve are leaders that are skilled at both.

The same is true here. There are brilliant, observant educators who have vast stores of knowledge, but who lack the skills to do anything with it. What kinds of skills are those? They are an eclectic mix of brains, tactics, diplomacy, motivation, cultural sensitivity, and plain old-fashioned political savvy and "people sense." Some leaders have these things; others do not. For those who do not, it's time to start working on them because our schools depend on them. Synthesizing and integrating these traits is a talent. Applying them is an art. Any artist will tell you that to develop a masterpiece of any kind takes patience, practice, and persistence. So does learning to be an advocate for the needs of all children and families. You do not just wake up one morning and say, "Gee, I think I will become an advocate for kids today. Maybe I'll just call up the governor and see if she wants to have breakfast. We could just meet out on the interstate, share a waffle, and change the world. I don't have anything else pressing to do today."

To become an advocate, you will need to work at it a little at a time, exhibit patience, practice what you are doing, and be persistent in developing activities and policies that will benefit all students and their families, inside and outside the school. You will have to work hard not just to be aware of trends, issues, and potential changes in the environment, but to talk about them in an intelligent manner. You will need to be in continuous discussion with all sorts of diverse groups within the school community about the potential impact they could have on schools and families. You cannot wait to see what happens because by then it could be too late. This means that above all, as an educational leader, you must have a voice and use it to advocate for policies and programs that promote equitable learning opportunities and success for all students, regardless of socioeconomic background, race, ethnicity, gender, language, or other individual characteristics. You cannot just advocate for the easy-to-teach, the likeable, or the college-bound. You must be the face and the voice for all students regardless of their circumstances. Following are two case studies that address the distinctions between knowledge and skills in their larger contexts to promote student success.

CASE STUDIES

Larger Context Knowledge: Schools Within a School

The learning community surrounding Hawthorne High School is concerned about the dropout rate among all students, but particularly those from underrepresented populations. For the last 3 years, multiple school and community leaders have been studying the issues, attempting to identify causes, investigating research from around the state and nation, and formulating possible ways to solve the dropout dilemma. They have uncovered significant research showing improved student performance—particularly for at-risk youth—at smaller high schools. Although controversial, the idea they would like to pursue is to divide the existing Hawthorne High School into four or five smaller "academies." These academies would be located on the same campus and share the same mascot, colors, and other unifying characteristics.

Each academy would have its own administrators, counselors, teachers, and support staff separate from the others. The specific distinguishing characteristic would be the theme of each academy. Students would apply and meet specific criteria for the individual academies within the larger school. In an effort to encourage and prepare learners to look ahead to a college experience, academies were projected around themes such as math and science, liberal arts, fine arts, cultural languages, and leadership. At the end of their first 2 years of high school, similar to the Oxford University model, every student would be required to produce and present a portfolio of their best work to a panel of community and school leaders who would subsequently help them individualize the remainder of their high school career. Junior and senior students would also be involved in the panel. Graduation would require successful completion of the collaboratively developed program of work, a significant community service project, and preparation of a lengthy paper that would synthesize and integrate the concepts and experiences they have learned and participated in during their academy experience. The goal of the "school within a school" is to identify and meet the individual interests and needs of students, as well as to encourage them to graduate from high school and continue with their education.

Although the school-within-a-school concept has tremendous support from most of the learning community, there are some who do not support it. There are concerns as to whether the school will receive adequate funding to accomplish it, how it will fit into local policies and state standards, and if every student will find his or her place and feel comfortable within the separate academies. Some feel its standards are so high that instead of encouraging students to stay in school, it will have the opposite effect and push them to drop out.

Reflective Analysis: Pause and Think

1. The school-within-a-school concept is generating considerable discussion. Based on research-based facts and examples, how could this concept be connected to the political, social, economic, legal, and cultural context of the students it expects to serve?

2. Provide examples of actual laws, policies, standards, curriculum guidelines, and graduation requirements in your district and state that would affect the development of a school within a school.

3. Develop a framework for a potential school within a school for your district. Include ramifications that address political, social, economic, legal, and cultural contexts.

4. Analyze, compare, and contrast the pros and cons of a school within a school within your community context. Draw conclusions based on the results.

5. Describe potential equity benefits and drawbacks for students participating in a school within a school on the academic, social, and psychological levels.

6. If you were appointed general administrator, charged with the organizational oversight of the entire school within a school, develop a strategic plan with specific points and explanations of how you would ensure equity of funds and resources for the entire operation.

Larger Context Skills: Title I

For many years, Joe Williamson Elementary School has been a Title I campus. This year preliminary data indicate the campus will not qualify for Title I funding. This data is partially indicated by a significant reduction of students on free and reduced lunch. Melda Guidry, principal of the school, is quite concerned about the negative impact this lack of funding will have on student programs and resources. She initiates an in-depth analysis with other staff members of indicators as to why this is occurring.

Their study shows that a major reason fewer students were qualifying for free and reduced lunch was because although the applications had been sent out, they were not being returned at rates similar to previous years. Upon further analysis, the committee learned that the primary source of unreturned applications was families whose native language was not English.

The Joe Williamson Campus Team devised a detailed plan to address the situation in a timely manner. This included resending applications with carefully worded instructions in the appropriate language. They made follow-up telephone calls in native languages when home phones were available. For those who still did not return their applications, faculty or staff members made home visits with interpreters. Other social service agencies that worked with the same families collaborated to see if they could help parents understand, complete, and return applications. Although this was a time-consuming process, the committee realized a significant increase in returned applications, primarily from the families of students who were likely to qualify for free or reduced lunch. Because of the staff and faculty's knowledge and application of political, social, economic, legal, and cultural mores and skills, the school created a "win–win" situation. More students were provided with the free or reduced-cost meals they needed, and the campus regained its Title I status and funding.

Reflective Analysis: Pause and Think

1. Research, describe, and summarize the criteria by which schools qualify for Title I assistance.

2. In what ways can Title I funds be used? What are the standards for use? Provide examples of ways Title I funds can and cannot be used.

3. In what manner should community input for campus Title I expenditures be developed, implemented, and evaluated?

4. Describe the process and ramifications for student and family assistance through the federal Free and Reduced Lunch Program.

5. Conceptualize and potentially lead a model of program evaluation for Title I programs at your campus (or another campus). Describe the research design, results of implementation, and recommendations for improvement.

6. Research and describe ways for to procure supplemental funds for a specific campus that does not qualify for Title I funding.

7. Analyze, compare, and contrast the benefits versus regulatory restraints of federal funds for campuses.

ACTIVITIES FOR PROFESSIONAL DEVELOPMENT

The principal should

- Explain the importance of using knowledge and personal skills as connections to improve community-based collaboratives and initiatives

- Research knowledge related to innovative school organizational structures that could benefit student learning for specific contextual situations
- Facilitate discussion and analysis among learning community members regarding unique organizational structures that could benefit student learning for their school
- Research the possible long- and short-term benefits and drawbacks of a school within a school
- Be well read on issues that relate (or could relate) to schools and learning; use professional journals, research-based literature, newspapers, news magazines, state and local newsletters, and Web sites
- Facilitate discussion among faculty and staff on the relevancy of advocacy including nonthreatening ways stakeholders can become or accelerate their efforts to be advocates for children
- Establish an advisory team made up of community leaders, social service agency representatives, parents, and other stakeholders to meet regularly and discuss current and potential issues that could affect the school learning environment
- Identify exemplary schools in similar settings (e.g., urban, suburban, rural, etc.) with similar demographics, and research factors that could be indicators of their success
- Set up visits to these campuses for self and other campus leaders to study the characteristics within their context
- Regularly recognize, reward, and celebrate the use of political, social, economic, legal, and cultural context skills resulting in student success within the learning community
- Provide training on ways to nurture and assist financially disadvantaged families
- Encourage faculty and staff to attend and participate in various community meetings and activities on issues that could impact students or families
- Host community meetings at the school so participants can visit the campus facilities, create valuable linkages, and improve community relationships
- Invite elected officials to visit the campus and speak to students and other community stakeholders on the benefits of

knowledge-based stewardship and unity of a vision of a growing, thriving learning community, focused on success for all members

In summary, educational leaders must have both the knowledge and skills to promote the success of all students. Knowledge is content oriented. Skills are application oriented, using knowledge we put into practice. It is possible to have knowledge of something without having the skill, talent, or desire to use it. To generate the success that all students need, educational leaders must have the knowledge, skills, and desire to be able to understand and influence the larger contexts discussed in Standard 6 that affect schools and families today.

CONCLUSIONS

Understanding these concepts is one thing; responding to them and influencing their outcomes are entirely different. Our goal is to do everything we can to make the world a better place. We do this by becoming proactive advocates for the needs of every child. If being a proactive advocate for all children is not our role, whose role is it? We are the school systems of the United States. It is our role, our duty, and our obligation to educate every child. Are you prepared? Begin now to do exactly that.

The Ultimate Application

1. Define and provide examples of a principal's role in incorporating political, social, economic, legal, and cultural contexts in applying school leadership.

2. Describe the community's perception of your school based on knowledge of how you and the school address the political, social, economic, legal, and cultural aspects of facilitating student success.

3. Develop a plan and timeline of things you as an educational leader could do to be more directly and indirectly involved in student and family advocacy.

4. Design a framework by which faculty, staff, and other learning community members could become involved in advocacy for student success within political, social, economic, legal, and cultural contexts.

5. Define and explain social justice. Develop activities for your campus that expand the development of social justice systems within your school and community.

6. Select a topic of interest, possibly a controversial one, in your school community. Prepare pros and cons for each side of the position based on generated data, policy, law, and other relevant factors for the contextual situation. Draw conclusions and make recommendations.

7. Develop campus-based activities to use the skills of the learning community relating to potential trends that could result in changes in the learning environment.

CHAPTER NINE

Trial By Fire

The Administrative Internship

STANDARD 7:

A school administrator is an educational leader who promotes the success of all students through substantial, sustained, standards-based experiences in real settings that are planned and guided cooperatively by university and school district personnel for graduate credit.

This standard has been the one to generate the most discussion among policymakers, professional organizations, practitioners, and universities. As the development and refinement of the standards progressed, the National Council for the Accreditation of Teacher Education (NCATE) and the Educational Leadership Constituent Council (ELCC) felt strongly that this standard on the importance of an authentic internship in real school settings was critical and must be included. The discussion focused on the ideal internship in multiple settings over a sustained period of time versus the practical difficulties that this could generate for students, universities, and school systems. In the end, the NCATE and the ELCC agreed that setting high standards for internships was the benchmark that would be most beneficial to all stakeholders.

If you are already an administrator, do not skip this chapter thinking it is not relevant to you. This isn't true for two reasons:

1. Just because you are already an administrator in no way means that you should stop growing and learning while performing your job. Administrators who no longer seek to learn, grow, synthesize, and apply what they have learned are no longer leaders. At best, they are managers. Regardless, they are not all they could be. All organizations obtain ultimate productivity only when their leaders continue to grow, learn, synthesize, and apply what they have learned.

2. The best school leaders are the ones who develop, nurture, and mentor others who will step forward in the future to join us in our quest to make the world a better place for children. To those wonderful human beings, I dedicate this chapter.

If you are a current educational leader, please find a future administrator to mentor and nurture based on these standards. Volunteer to collaborate with a university preparation program to identify the best and the brightest for school leadership—the noblest of callings.

If you are a current or potential student, professor, or university administrator, take heed to the criteria specified in Standard 7. Restructure your programs, be creative, and think outside the box so that your students can have a substantial, sustained, standards-based internship experience. Develop something no one has done before. Do what others say cannot be done. Anything is possible with enough time and with collaborative, collective minds working together to create something better than any of us could have imagined. The internship standard does not prescribe how all programs should look; it does describe common core components that quality programs should contain.

PHILOSOPHICAL FRAMEWORK

A Substantial Internship Experience

The internship should be substantial. It should not be something students piece together in the hours before or after school or something from which they gain no true experience in applying knowledge and skills in the role of the administrator. Internship activities should be authentic. They should involve things real administrators do each day rather than busy work a mentor has delegated to interns that requires no synthesis or application of true leadership concepts. I once knew an intern who was directed to do cafeteria duty and then told to help wipe down the tables after the students left. When the intern questioned whether this was in fact a substantial leadership development activity, he was told that all administrators help with this duty, and he should, too. This may be true, but it would be difficult to directly connect this activity to one of these standards. What merit to his maturation as a campus leader did it provide? None. Instead, it led to university intervention to clarify and define the partnership responsibilities of the school, the university, and the intern. The goal was to facilitate his acquiring experience in skills that provide leadership training rather than crowd control or table wiping.

The ideal situation (such as the Educational Leadership UTA program at the University of Texas at Arlington) is a full-time, year-long, paid internship conducted under a trained mentor with joint supervision from school district and university personnel (Wilmore, 1999, 2000; Wilmore & McNeil, 1999; Wilmore & Thomas, 1998). Unfortunately, the ideal is not always possible. Standard 7 suggests a 6-month or equivalent full-time mentored experience, preferably involving two or more school and community settings with students at multiple levels and of various ages. Universities have freedom and flexibility to create programs that contain these components and that meet the needs of their constituencies. Creativity and a positive attitude are the key building blocks to overcoming barriers to success.

A Sustained Internship Experience

The internship should be a sustained experience that takes place over an extended period of time near the completion of the program. It should allow for application of skills and knowledge on a full-time basis. The activities in which the intern participates should be collaboratively planned between the intern, the university supervisor, and the district supervisor. Activities should be structured to meet the dual needs of the intern and the campus and should also be directly correlated to the standards. Most important, activities should not be random but should have a focus and purpose directed toward school improvement, renewal, and student success. This is easier said than done when interns usually having full-time jobs as teachers during the day and are trying to squeeze in internship hours to meet university requirements whenever possible. What can they learn from that? Nothing. This is the purpose of Standard 7. By sustaining the internship from 6 months to a year of full-time, standards-based experiences rather than a shorter term, random mix of unrelated experiences, the student has the opportunity to integrate research-based knowledge and theories in a safe, structured learning environment.

A Standards-Based Internship Experience

All internship experiences should be connected to state or national professional standards, not to randomly selected and implemented standards. By using research-based and collaboratively developed standards, internship experiences have a framework around which they can be developed and focused. The standards provide meaningful constructs. Although planning these experiences will be more time-consuming to develop, implement, and assess, the result will be an authentic internship experience. Because of this additional thought and effort from all members of the collaborative team, the intern will be better prepared to lead and advance learning for others. Although time-consuming, connecting all learning activities to the standards creates a multiple "win–win" situation for all stakeholders.

Real Settings

The ideal situation is for the internship to occur in multiple school and community settings and at multiple age levels. In reality, this could become a logistical nightmare for universities and school districts as they try to place the interns. But aside from the logistics involved, think how wonderful it would be if every intern that came through every NCATE-accredited program in school leadership had internship experiences in at least one elementary, one intermediate or middle school, and one high school, and—even better—if every intern was able to experience some form of alternative school setting from an administrative perspective. Think how wonderful it would be if every intern also had the opportunity to work closely with at least one social service agency, tying the concept of collaboration to the reality of actually doing it in the real world. Think how wonderful it would be if every intern also got to work hand in hand with a local business to see how leadership is facilitated in a for-profit organization. Compare the richness and diversity of those potential contextual experiences with the chemistry teacher trying to fit in random internship hours during his or her conference period, before and after school, or during lunch. The difference is about as stark as the Swiss mountains versus the Sahara Desert. This contrast speaks for itself in presenting the case for using creativity in program development or revision and overcoming any logistical difficulties. Students receive a richer contextual experience in multiple, real, and diverse settings that better prepares them for their roles as true leaders of the entire school community.

To implement the concepts described here, school districts, universities, and other preparation programs must give new meaning to the ideas of creative problem solving and thinking outside the box. Will this be a difficult task? Obviously. But could it result in innovative programs that are standards based and designed to prepare administrators who are ready to meet the challenges the future holds? Definitely.

We said earlier that there are no easy answers to the daunting tasks school leaders face. Things are rarely simple, or cut and dried. In-depth problems require in-depth study, research, and brainstorming; they require tons of discussion, trial and error, piloting, evaluation, and so forth. The list goes on forever. In the same way, humans did not walk on the moon the day after someone decided to try. It took vision, foresight, research, planning, assessments, and hard work. So does quality school leadership preparation. It is time to get out of our comfort zones, revisit, revise, and update old paradigms and do what we can to improve the world through improved school leadership preparation. We do this one intern at a time.

Planned and Guided
Cooperatively for Graduate Credit

This standard sets high expectations for integrating and implementing each of the others. No longer can administrative interns be sent into the schools to get their required hours as best they can as independent units, do "busy work" or disjointed activities for their principals, and hope they are getting the right opportunities to fulfill university requirements. This standard sets the parameters for a full, well-rounded, balanced, and standards-based experience. All stakeholders must become invested in the growth of the intern by working and planning coordinated activities to ensure an optimal experience. Each activity the intern undertakes must be planned by the student, his or her site supervisor, and a university representative. This triad, and perhaps others, works collaboratively to provide and assess quality opportunities for the intern in which to apply knowledge, skills, and research in schools. A plan should be prepared that will address the intern's strengths and weakness while systematically addressing how each will be developed, nurtured, and sustained for maximum intern growth and productivity. Thus each intern should be provided with a trained mentor who will invest time, energy, and commitment to his or her growth and development. These mentors should be successful principals; interns should not be placed in situations to "shore up" less-than-adequate administrators. Individual, campus, and program goals should be identified early in the process with strategic activities planned to target their attainment. When the triad works, plans, and guides the process and any products developed during the internship, the candidate achieves maximum growth opportunities. All of this must occur with the student gaining supervised graduate credit toward his or her program of study.

CONCLUSIONS

Developing substantial, sustained, standards-based internships in real settings will require patience, practice, and perseverance. We may not get it right the first time, but we will keep assessing, modifying, and improving until someday soon all interns have the opportunity to test their wings in a safe and supported opportunity that is full-time, field-based, and sustained over a significant period. Until then, we must keep taking steps in the right direction to provide the best possible experiences we can, each day looking to make student opportunities richer and more diverse. This is what they deserve. This is what the schools they will serve deserve. This is what society as a whole deserves. It is up to us to provide it.

PART THREE

Conclusions

CHAPTER TEN

The Hallelujah Chorus
Tying It Together to Transform the Learning Community

We have worked our way through six standards that directly relate to the research and knowledge base of creating successful school leaders and one standard on the characteristics of an ideal internship experience. We have analyzed case studies for each component of the standards, asked critical questions, and looked at extensive potential professional development activities for future and current principals. Now that we know and understand the standards, how do we go about applying them for the success of all students?

FINAL REVIEW

Every one of these standards is excellent. Let's briefly review them and the concepts they represent.

A school administrator is an educational leader who promotes the success of all students by

- Standard 1: *facilitating the development, articulation, implementation, and stewardship of a school or district vision of learning that is shared and supported by the school community.*

It is the role of the principal to work collaboratively with all stake-holders to develop a shared and supported campus vision of where the school community wants to be rather than where it is. It is imperative that multiple stakeholders participate in the development process. People support what they help to build. Once the vision is developed, it must be articulated (communicated and marketed) and implemented (put into action). It is the responsibility of the principal to be a prudent steward of the vision within the school community by being the voice of and advocate for the value of education for all learners.

- Standard 2: *advocating, nurturing, and sustaining a school culture and instructional program conducive to student learning and staff professional growth.*

Culture is a comprehensive term that includes the way things are done as well as what is valued on a campus. It advocates the heritage and traditions of the school. Furthermore, it feeds and supports a climate that is valued, rewarded, and celebrated and that contributes to the way the school nurtures and supports its learning environment. The principal must advocate, nurture, and sustain the school culture, its instructional programs, and the community such that they are learner centered and facilitate both student and staff growth.

- Standard 3: *ensuring management of the organization, operations, and resources for a safe, efficient, and effective learning environment.*

If facilities are not safe, efficient, and effective for learning, they really do not deserve to be called schools nor do their administrators deserve to be called educational leaders. It is the responsibility of the principal to ensure the school is operated in a prudent manner that supports the learning environment for all stakeholders. This is a management-versus-leadership issue that ensures the safe, efficient, and effective operation of the school so that teachers can teach and students can learn.

- Standard 4: *collaborating with families and community members, responding to diverse community interests and needs, and mobilizing community resources.*

The principal is the tie that binds the school together and who extends that bond to include families and other community members to form a collaborative team. The single focus of this team is a common vision of student success. The purpose is to respond to the many diverse needs and interests within the community and to mobilize the necessary resources to meet them. The principal provides the organizational oversight as well as personal, campus, and community sensitivity to align needs, interests, and resources.

- Standard 5: *acting with integrity, fairness, and in an ethical manner.*

If principals expect members of the school community to act with integrity and fairness and in an ethical manner, then they must practice what they preach. Their lives must mirror the values they espouse. Principals must be effective character role models in the schools and in the community. Everyone's eyes are on them. All people must be treated with integrity, fairness, and in an ethical manner. All principals must conduct themselves with integrity and fairness and in an ethical manner at all times, even when it is difficult.

- Standard 6: *understanding, responding to, and influencing the larger political, social, economic, legal, and cultural context.*

Principals must be knowledgeable about the many diverse influences that affect the school and also must have the skills to use that knowledge for the benefit of children and families. The principal is the school's primary voice and its advocate for children. Principals therefore must take a proactive role at the local, state, and national levels to facilitate laws and policies that benefit children. To meet this requirement, principals must be well read, be well versed on current events, and be proactive to new or potential legislation, regulations, or policies that could affect teaching and learning in any way.

- Standard 7: *through substantial, sustained, standards-based experiences in real settings that are planned and guided cooperatively by university and school district personnel for graduate credit.*

An internship is the primary forum in which future administrators can apply their knowledge. Internships should take place in supportive, safe arenas, preferably in multiple pre-kindergarten through 12th-grade settings and with a coordinated experience in some form of social service agency. These experiences must be authentic, substantial, sustained, based on standards, and conducted in real settings over an extended period of time. These experiences cannot occur in segments in which students attempt as best they can to practice what they have learned in a uncoordinated manner. Internships must be jointly planned, implemented, and assessed by school, community, and university personnel. The support of the internship thus becomes a coordinated team effort where all stakeholders become winners. This is why it is crucial that interns have nurturing, learning relationships with trained mentors who are solid educational leaders. They should also work with university and other district and community personnel, such as individuals from business and industry, social service agencies, or any other arena where students can be exposed to and participate in diverse forms of organizational leadership and where both units can benefit. In an ideal situation, all interns would have a sustained, nurturing, and supportive full-time internship. It would be spread over an entire year so they could see the opening and closing of the school year as well as everything in between. It would take place in multiple school settings and include experiences in noneducational organizations so they could benefit from diverse leadership styles and perspectives. Just imagine what a fuller, richer, and more meaningful experience it would be for future administrators, schools, and the community we serve if all interns could benefit from this form of standards-based internship.

CONCLUSIONS

For any one human to accomplish all the complexities of these standards may seem as difficult as walking on water. Nonetheless, it is exceedingly important to have solid, research-based standards to strive for. Remember how we started with Les Brown's concept of reaching for the moon? Even if you miss it, you'll land among the stars. This is what these standards are all about. They set very high expectations. Not everyone will reach them all the time. But they are benchmarks to reach for. Even if we cannot achieve them in every instance, our achievement will be higher than if we had no goals. It is my firm and committed desire that every one of us strive for and reach the moon as we go after these new standards in a focused and systematic manner. America's school children deserve nothing less.

APPLAUSE!

Many stakeholders are to be applauded. National Council for the Accreditation of Teacher Education, Interstate School Leaders Licensure Consortium, Educational Leadership Constituent Council, National Policy Board for Educational Administration, Council of Chief State School Officers, and all the professional organizations, professors, practitioners, and others who have worked to reach collaborative synthesis and agreement on this comprehensive set of standards. Each of these groups has provided a service far beyond the call of duty. The benefits of these standards will be far-reaching and enduring. Thank you for your vision, purpose, patience, and persistence as you have sought to advance the cause of improved school leadership preparation and to have a positive impact on society.

GO FORTH AND DO WELL!

It is up to the rest of us to roll up our sleeves, integrate the standards, revamp programs, and continue the never-ending process of dialogue and collaboration that is necessary to perpetuate the process of change and improvement. We must continue to develop partnerships between schools, higher education, professional organizations, social service agencies, businesses, churches, and the rest of the learning community for the common purpose of student success and an improved democratic society. Together we are very powerful. We must use this power as advocates for all children. If we don't, who will?

School leadership is a calling. Some people have it; some do not. To have it is a gift. No one receives a beautiful present and then leaves it carefully wrapped in its box. It's time to open our gifts and share them with others. To go forward, you must be called to school leadership as your mission. Pursue it with every ounce of passion and vigor you possess. It is your gift. Please do not fail to open it. The ELCC standards provide a framework and a mechanism from which to work. Use them to develop strategies to make your campus, community, or university a better place. Now, go forth and make a difference in the future of our society—one student and school at a time. The standards are our framework. They are a base for creativity and innovation in leadership and leadership preparation. Through these standards, you can make a difference. We can do it together. Let's do it well.

Suggested Additional Reading

This list is not intended to be an exhaustive guide, but a source of supplemental reading that supports the concepts presented in the ELCC standards. Most of these resources include content that is relevant to more than one standard.

STANDARD 1

Bennis, W. (1989). *Why leaders can't lead.* San Francisco: Jossey-Bass.

Blanchard, K., & Bowles, S. (1998). *Gung-ho!* New York: William Morrow.

Blanchard, K., Hybels, B., & Hodges, P. (1999). *Leadership by the book: Tools to transform your workplace.* New York: William Morrow.

Bolman, L. G., & Deal, T. E. (1997). *Reframing organizations: Artistry, choice, and leadership* (2nd ed.). San Francisco: Jossey-Bass.

Bolman, L. G., & Deal, T. E. (2001). *Leading with soul: An uncommon journey of spirit.* San Francisco: Jossey-Bass.

Brock, B. L., & Grady, M. L. (2000). *Rekindling the flame.* Thousand Oaks, CA: Corwin.

De Pree, M. (1989). *Leadership is an art.* New York: Dell.

DeWitt Wallace-Reader's Digest Fund Study Conference. (1992). *Developing a framework for the continual professional development of administrators in the northeast.* (ERIC Document Reproduction Service No. ED383104).

Fullan, M. (2001). *Leading in a culture of change.* San Francisco: Jossey-Bass.

Hoyle, J. (1995). *Leadership and futuring: Making visions happen.* Thousand Oaks, CA: Corwin.

Hoyle, J. (2001). *Leadership and the force of love: Six keys to motivating with love.* Thousand Oaks, CA: Corwin.

Johnson, S. (1998). *Who moved my cheese?* New York: Putnam.

Kouzes, J. M., & Posner, B. Z. (1998). *Encouraging the heart: A leader's guide to rewarding and recognizing others.* San Francisco: Jossey-Bass.

Krzyzewski, M., & Phillips, D. T. (2000). *Leading with the heart: Coach K's successful strategies for basketball, business, and life.* New York: Warner Business Books.

Maxwell, J. C. (1995). *Developing the leaders around you.* Nashville, TN: Thomas Nelson.

Peters, T., & Waterman, R. H. (1993). *In search of excellence.* New York: Warner Books.

Ramsey, R. D. (1999). *Lead, follow, or get out of the way.* Thousand Oaks, CA: Corwin.

Sergiovanni, T. J. (2001). *The principalship: A reflective practice perspective* (4th ed.). Needham Heights, MA: Allyn & Bacon.

STANDARD 2

Banks, J. A., & Banks, C. M. (1996). *Multicultural education: Issues and perspectives.* Boston: Allyn & Bacon.

Barker, C. L., & Searchwell, C. J. (1998). *Writing meaningful teacher evaluations—right now!!* Thousand Oaks, CA: Corwin.

Barker, C. L., & Searchwell, C. J. (2001). *Writing year-end teacher improvement plans—right now!!* Thousand Oaks, CA: Corwin.

Beach, D. M., & Reinhartz, J. (2000). *Supervisory leadership.* Boston: Allyn & Bacon.

Beane, J. A. (1997). *Curriculum integration: Designing the core of democratic education.* New York: Teachers College Press.

Bigge, M. L., & Shermis, S. S. (1999). *Learning theories for teachers* (6th ed.). New York: Addison-Wesley Longman.

Blanchard, K., & Johnson, S. (1981). *The one minute manager.* New York: Berkley.

Blase, J., & Kirby, P. C. (1992). *Bringing out the best in teachers: What effective principals do.* Newbury Park, CA: Corwin.

Bocchino, R. (1999). *Emotional literacy: To be a different kind of smart.* Thousand Oaks, CA: Corwin.

Bolman, L., & Deal, T. (1995). *The path to school leadership.* Thousand Oaks, CA: Corwin.

Bracey, G. W. (2000). *Bail me out! Handling difficult data and tough questions about public schools.* Thousand Oaks, CA: Corwin.

Brewer, E. W., DeJonge, J. O., & Stout, V. J. (2001). *Moving online: Making the transition from traditional instruction and communication strategies.* Thousand Oaks, CA: Corwin.

Bucher, R. D. (2000). *Diversity consciousness: Opening our minds to people, cultures, and opportunities.* Upper Saddle River, NJ: Prentice Hall.

Burrello, L. C., Lashley, C., & Beatty, E. E. (2001). *Educating all students together: How school leaders create unified systems.* Thousand Oaks, CA: Corwin.

Burton, V. R. (2000). *Rich minds, rich rewards.* Dallas, TX: Pearl.

Carbo, M. (2000). *What every principal should know about teaching reading.* Syosset, NY: National Reading Styles Institute.

Costa, A. L., & Garmston, R. J. (1994). *Cognitive coaching.* Norwood, MA: Christopher Gordon.

Creighton, T. B. (2000). *The educator's guide for using data to improve decision making.* Thousand Oaks, CA: Corwin.

Crow, G. M., & Matthews, L. J. (1998). *Finding one's way: How mentoring can lead to dynamic leadership.* Thousand Oaks, CA: Corwin.

Danielson, C., & McGreal, T. L. (2000). *Teacher evaluation to enhance professional practice.* Princeton, NJ: Educational Testing Service.

Daresh, J. (2001). *Leaders helping leaders: A practical guide to administrative mentoring* (2nd ed.). Thousand Oaks, CA: Corwin.

Deal, T. E., & Peterson, K. D. (1994). *The leadership paradox.* San Francisco: Jossey-Bass.

Deal, T. E., & Peterson, K. D. (1999). *Shaping school culture: The heart of leadership.* San Francisco: Jossey-Bass.

English, F. W. (2000). *Deciding what to teach and test: Developing, aligning, and auditing the curriculum* (Millennium Ed.). Thousand Oaks, CA: Corwin.

Glanz, J. (1998). *Action research: An educational guide to school improvement.* Norwood, MA: Christopher Gordan.

Glatthorn, A. A. (2001). *The principal as curriculum leader* (2nd ed.). Thousand Oaks, CA: Corwin.

Glenn, H. S., & Brock, M. L. (1998). *7 strategies for developing capable students.* Roseville, CA: Prima.

Gregory, G. H., & Chapman, C. (2001). *Differentiated instructional strategies: One size doesn't fit all.* Thousand Oaks, CA: Corwin.

Hadaway, N., Vardell, S. M., & Young, T. (2001). *Literature-based instruction with English language learners.* Boston: Allyn & Bacon.

Holcomb, E. L. (1998). *Getting excited about data: How to combine people, passion, and proof.* Thousand Oaks, CA: Corwin.

Hoyle, J. H., English, F., & Steffy, B. (1998). *Skills for successful 21st century school leaders.* Arlington, VA: American Association of School Administrators.

Joyce, B., & Weil, M. (1996). *Models of teaching.* Needham Heights, MA: Simon & Schuster.

Kozol, J. (1992). *Savage inequalities: Children in America's schools.* New York: Harper Perennial Library.

Kozol, J. (2000). *Ordinary resurrections: Children in the years of hope.* New York: Crown.

Leithwood K., Aitken, R., & Jantzi, D. (2001). *Making schools smarter: A system for monitoring school and district progress* (2nd ed.). Thousand Oaks, CA: Corwin.

Oliva, P. F. (1997). *Supervision in today's schools* (5th ed.). New York: John Wiley.

Payne, R. K. (1998). *A framework for understanding poverty.* Baytown, TX: RFT.

Pratt, D. (1994). *Curriculum planning: A handbook for professionals*: Ft. Worth, TX: Harcourt Brace College.

Reksten, L. E. (2000). *Using technology to increase student learning*. Thousand Oaks, CA: Corwin.

Schlechty, P. C. (2001). *Shaking up the school house*. San Francisco: Jossey-Bass.

Sergiovanni, T. J., & Starratt, R. J. (1998). *Supervision: A redefinition* (6th ed.). Boston: McGraw-Hill.

Thompson, S. J., Quenemoen, R. F., Thurlow, M. L., & Ysseldyke, J. E. (2001). *Alternate assessments for students with disabilities*. Thousand Oaks, CA: Corwin.

Thurlow, M. L., Elliott, J. L. & Ysseldyke, J. E. (1998). *Testing students with disabilities: Practical strategies for complying with district and state requirements*. Thousand Oaks, CA: Corwin.

Weil, J., Weil B., & Weil, M. (1998). *Models of teaching* (6th ed.). Needham Neights, MA: Simon & Schuster.

Whitaker, T. (1999). *Dealing with difficult teachers*. Larchmont, NY: Eye on Education.

Woodward, J., & Cuban, L. (Eds.). (2001). *Technology, curriculum, and professional development: Adapting schools to meet the needs of students with disabilities*. Thousand Oaks, CA: Corwin.

Worthen, B., Sanders, J., & Fitzpatrick, J. (1996). *Program evaluation, alternative approaches and practical guidelines* (2nd ed.). New York: Addison-Wesley.

STANDARD 3

Anderson, J. W. (2001). *The answers to questions that teachers most frequently ask*. Thousand Oaks, CA: Corwin.

Bennis, W. (1997). *Managing people is like herding cats*. Provo, UT: Executive Excellence.

Brewer, E. W., Achilles, C. M., Fuhriman, J. R., & Hollingsworth, C. (2001). *Finding funding: Grantwriting from start to finish, including project management and internet use*. Thousand Oaks, CA: Corwin.

Burrup, P. E., Brimpley, V., Jr., & Garfield, R. R. (1998). *Financing education in a climate of change* (7th ed.). Boston: Allyn & Bacon.

Coleman, M., & Anderson, L. (2000). *Managing finance and resources in education.* Thousand Oaks, CA: Corwin.

DiGiulio, R. C. (2001). *Educate, medicate, or litigate? What teachers, parents, and administrators must do about student behavior.* Thousand Oaks, CA: Corwin.

Dyer, K. M. (2000). *The intuitive principal.* Thousand Oaks, CA: Corwin.

Erlandson, D. A., Stark, P. L., & Ward, S. M. (1996). *Organizational oversight: Planning and scheduling for effectiveness.* Larchmont, NY: Eye on Education.

Ledeen, M. A. (1999). *Machiavelli on modern leadership.* New York: St. Martin's Press.

Lunenburg, F. C., & Ornstein, A. C. (2000). *Educational administration: Concepts and practices* (3rd ed.). Belmont, CA: Wadsworth/Thomas Learning.

McNamara, J. F., Erlandson, D. A., & McNamara, M. (1999). *Measurement and evaluation: Strategies for school improvement.* Larchmont, NY: Eye on Education.

Odden, A., & Archibald, S. (2001). *Reallocating resources: How to boost student achievement without asking for more.* Thousand Oaks, CA: Corwin.

Parsons, B. A. (2001). *Evaluative inquiry: Using evaluation to promote student success.* Thousand Oaks, CA: Corwin.

Peterson, S. (2001). *The grantwriter's internet companion: A resource for educators and others seeking grants and funding.* Thousand Oaks, CA: Corwin.

Ramsey, R. D. (2001). *Fiscal fitness for school administrators: How to stretch resources and do even more with less.* Thousand Oaks, CA: Corwin.

Sanders, J. R. (2000). *Evaluating school programs* (2nd ed.). Thousand Oaks, CA: Corwin.

Schmieder, J. H., & Cairns, D. (1996). *Ten skills of highly effective principals.* Lancaster, PA: Technomic.

Sergiovanni, T. J. (2000). *The lifeworld of leadership.* San Francisco: Jossey-Bass.

Slavin, R. E., & Fashola, O. S. (1998). *Show me the evidence! Proven and promising programs for America's schools.* Thousand Oaks, CA: Corwin.

Smith, H. W. (1994). *The 10 natural laws of successful time and life management.* New York: Warner Books.

STANDARD 4

Batey, C. S. (1996). *Parents are lifesavers: A handbook for parent involvement in schools.* Thousand Oaks, CA: Corwin.

Bennis, W. (1999). *Old dogs, new tricks.* Provo, UT: Executive Excellence.

Burke, M. A., & Picus, L. O. (2001). *Developing community-empowered schools.* Thousand Oaks, CA: Corwin.

De Pree, M. (1997). *Leading without power: Finding hope in serving community.* San Francisco: Jossey-Bass.

Decker, R. H. (1997). *When a crisis hits: Will your school be ready?* Thousand Oaks, CA: Corwin.

Doyle, D. P., & Pimentel, S. (1999). *Raising the standard: An eight-step action guide for schools and communities.* Thousand Oaks, CA: Corwin.

Drucker Foundation. (1996). *The leader of the future.* San Francisco: Jossey-Bass.

Dyer, K. M., & Carothers, J. (2000). *The intuitive principal: A guide to leadership.* Thousand Oaks, CA: Corwin.

Epstein, J. L., Coates, L., Salinas, K. C., Sanders, M. G., & Simon, B. S. (1997). *School, family, and community partnerships: Your handbook for action.* Thousand Oaks, CA: Corwin.

Holcomb, E. L. (2001). *Asking the right questions: Techniques for collaboration and school change* (2nd ed.). Thousand Oaks, CA: Corwin.

Jayanthi, M., & Nelson, J. S. (2001). *Savvy decision making: An administrator's guide to using focus groups in schools.* Thousand Oaks, CA: Corwin.

Kaser, J., Mundry, S., Stiles, K. E., Loucks-Horsley, S. (2001). *Leading every day: 124 actions for effective leadership.* Thousand Oaks, CA: Corwin.

Kosmoski, G. J., & Pollack, D. R. (2000). *Managing difficult, frustrating, and hostile conversations: Strategies for savvy administrators.* Thousand Oaks, CA: Corwin.

McEwan, E. K. (1997). *Leading your team to excellence: How to make quality decisions.* Thousand Oaks, CA: Corwin.

Seiler, T. L. (2001). *Developing your case for support.* San Francisco: Jossey-Bass.

Thomas, S. J. (1999). *Designing surveys that work! A step-by-step guide.* Thousand Oaks, CA: Corwin.

Trump, K. S. (1998). *Practical school security: Basic guidelines for safe and secure schools.* Thousand Oaks, CA: Corwin.

Veale, J. R., Morley, R. E., & Erickson, C. L. (2001). *Practical evaluation for collaborative services: Goals, processes, tools, and reporting systems for school-based programs.* Thousand Oaks, CA: Corwin.

Wachter, J. C. (1999). *Classroom volunteers: Uh-Oh! Or Right On!* Thousand Oaks, CA: Corwin.

Whitaker, T. A., Whitaker, B., & Lumpa, D. (2000). *Motivating & inspiring teachers: The educational leader's guide for building staff morale.* Larchmont, NY: Eye on Education.

STANDARD 5

Blanchard, K., Oncken, W., Jr., & Burrows, H. (1989). *The one minute manager meets the monkey.* New York: William Morrow.

Blanchard, K., & Peale, N. V. (1988). *The power of ethical management.* New York: Fawcett Columbine.

Blanchard, K., Zigarmi, P., & Zigmari, D. (1985). *Leadership and the one minute manager.* New York: William Morrow.

Dunklee, D. R. (2000). *If you want to lead, not just manage: A primer for principals.* Thousand Oaks, CA: Corwin.

Gray, K. C. (1999). *Getting real: Helping teens find their future.* Thousand Oaks, CA: Corwin.

Josephson, M. S., & Hanson, W. (1998). *The power of character.* San Francisco: Jossey-Bass.

Osier, J. L. & Fox, H. P. (2001). *Settle conflicts right now! A step-by-step guide for K-6 classrooms.* Thousand Oaks, CA: Corwin.

Pellicer, L. O. (1999). *Caring enough to lead: Schools and the sacred trust.* Thousand Oaks, CA: Corwin.

Podesta, C. (1993). *Self-esteem and the 6-second secret* (updated edition). Newbury Park, CA: Corwin.

Podesta, C., & Sanderson, V. (1999). *Life would be easy if it weren't for other people.* Thousand Oaks, CA: Corwin.

Sergiovanni, T. J. (1992). *Moral leadership: Getting to the heart of school improvement.* San Francisco: Jossey-Bass.

Snowden, P. E., & Gorton, R. A. (1998). *School leadership and administration: Important concepts, case studies, and simulations* (5th ed.). New York: McGraw-Hill.

York-Barr, J., Sommers, W. A., Ghere, G. S., & Montie, J. (2001). *Reflective practice to improve schools: An action guide for educators.* Thousand Oaks, CA: Corwin.

STANDARD 6

Covey, S. R. (1990). *Principle-centered leadership.* New York: Simon & Schuster.

Covey, S. R. (1990). *The seven habits of highly effective people.* New York: Simon & Schuster.

Covey, S. R., Merrill, A. R., & Merrill, R. R. (1994). *First things first.* New York: Simon & Schuster.

Dunklee, D. R., & Shoop, R. J. (2001). *The principal's quick-reference guide to school law: reducing liability, litigation, and other potential legal tangles.* Thousand Oaks, CA: Corwin.

English, F. W. (1994). *Theory in educational administration.* New York: HarperCollins.

Hoy, W. H., & Miskel, C. G. (1996). *Educational administration: Theory, research, and practice* (5th ed.). New York: McGraw-Hill.

Palestini, R. H. (1999). *Educational administration: Leading with mind and heart.* Lancaster, PA: Technomic.

Reagan, T. G., Case, C. W., & Brubacher, J. W. (2000). *Becoming a reflective educator: How to build a culture of inquiry in the schools.* Thousand Oaks, CA: Corwin.

Reinhartz, J., & Beach, D. M. (2001). *Foundations of educational leadership: Changing schools, changing roles.* Boston: Allyn & Bacon.

Schumaker, D. R., & Sommers, W. A. (2001). *Being a successful principal: Riding the wave of change without drowning.* Thousand Oaks, CA: Corwin.

Skrla, L., Erlandson, D. A., Reed, E. M., & Wilson, A. P. (2001). *The emerging principalship.* Larchmont, NY: Eye on Education.

Sperry, D. J. (1999). *Working in a legal and regulatory environment: A handbook for school leaders.* Larchmont, NY: Eye on Education.

Streshly, W. A. Walsh, J., & Frase, L. E. (2001). *Avoiding legal hassles: What school administrators really need to know* (2nd ed.). Thousand Oaks, CA: Corwin.

Thomson, S. (Ed.). (1993). *Principals of our changing schools: Knowledge and skill base.* Alexandria, VA: National Policy Board for Educational Administration.

STANDARD 7

Alvy, H. B., & Robbins, P. (1998). *If I only knew . . . Success strategies for navigating the principalship.* Thousand Oaks, CA: Corwin.

Brown, G., & Irby, B. (2001). *The principal portfolio* (2nd ed.). Thousand Oaks, CA: Corwin.

Capasso, R. L., & Daresh, J. C. (2001). *The school administrator internship handbook: Leading, mentoring, and participating in the internship program.* Thousand Oaks, CA: Corwin.

Daresh, J. (2001). *What it means to be a principal: Your guide to leadership.* Thousand Oaks, CA: Corwin.

Daresh, J., & Playco, M. (2001). *Beginning the principalship: A practical guide for new school leaders* (2nd ed.). Thousand Oaks, CA: Corwin.

Hartzell, G. N., Williams, R. C., & Nelson, K. T. (1995). *New voices in the field: The work lives of first-year assistant principals.* Thousand Oaks, CA: Corwin.

Irby, B. J., & Brown, G. (2000). *The career advancement portfolio.* Thousand Oaks, CA: Corwin.

Robbins, P., & Alvy, H. B. (1995). *The principal's companion: Strategies and hints to make the job easier.* Thousand Oaks, CA: Corwin.

Sharp, W. L., Walter, J. K., & Sharp, H. M. (1998). *Case studies for school leaders: Implementing the ISLLC standards.* Lancaster, PA: Technomic.

Villani, S. (1999). *Are you sure you're the principal? On being an authentic leader.* Thousand Oaks, CA: Corwin.

Wyatt, R. L., III, & Looper, S. (2000). *So you have to have a portfolio: A teacher's guide to preparation and presentation.* Thousand Oaks, CA: Corwin.

References

Blanchard, K., & Bowles, S. (1998). *Gung-ho!* New York: William Morrow.

Blanchard, K., & Johnson, S. (1982). *The one-minute manager.* New York: Berkley.

Burton, V. (1999). *Rich minds, rich rewards.* Dallas, TX: Pearl Books.

Council of Chief State School Officers. (1996). *Interstate school leaders licensure consortium: Standards for school leaders.* Washington, DC: Author.

Covey, S. R. (1990a). *Principle-centered leadership.* New York: Simon & Schuster.

Covey, S. R. (1990b). *The seven habits of highly effective people.* New York: Simon and Schuster.

Covey, S. R., Merrill, A. R., & Merrill, R. R. (1994). *First things first.* New York: Simon & Schuster.

Deal, T. E., & Peterson, K. D. (1994). *The leadership paradox.* San Francisco: Jossey-Bass.

Deal, T. E., & Peterson, K. D. (1999). *Shaping school culture: The heart of leadership.* San Francisco: Jossey-Bass.

Fenwick, L. T., & Pierce, M. C. (2001). The principal shortage: Crisis or opportunity? *Principal, 80*(4), 24–28.

Glanz, J. (1998). *Action research: An educational guide to school improvement.* Norwood, MA: Christopher Gordan.

Haertel, E. H. (1999). Performance assessment and educational reform. *Phi Delta Kappan, 80,* 662–666.

Hoyle, J. R., English, F. W., & Steffy, B. E. (1998). *Skills for successful 21st century school leaders: Standards for peak performers.* Arlington, VA: American Association of School Administrators.

Johnson, S. (1998). *Who moved my cheese?* New York: Putnam.

Lashway, L. (2001, Summer). The state of standards. *Research Roundup, 17,* 4.

Maxwell, J. C. (1995). *Developing the leaders around you.* Nashville, TN: Thomas Nelson.

McCown, C., Arnold, M., Miles, D., & Hargadine, K. (2000). Why principals succeed: Comparing principal performance to national professional standards. *ERS Spectrum, 18*(2), 14–19.

McNeil, L. (2000). Creating new inequalities: Contradictions of reform. *Phi Delta Kappan, 81,* 728–734.

Million, J. (1998, April). Where have all the principals gone? *NAESP Communicator, 21,* 5.

Murphy, J., & Shipman, N. J. (1998). *The interstate school leaders licensure consortium: A standards-based approach to strengthening educational leadership.* Paper presented to the annual conference of the American Educational Research Association, San Diego, CA.

Murphy, J., Shipman, N. J., & Pearlman, M. (1997). Strengthening educational leadership: The ISLLC standards. *Streamlined Seminar, 16*(1), 1–4.

Murphy, J., Yff, J., & Shipman, N. J. (2000). Implementation of the interstate school leaders licensure consortium standards. *International Journal of Leadership in Education, 3*(1), 17–39.

National Commission on Excellence in Education. (1983, April). *A nation at risk: The imperative for educational reform.* Retrieved December 15, 2001 from http://www.ed.gov/pubs/ NatAtRisk/index.html

National Policy Board for Educational Administration. (2001). *Advanced programs in educational leadership for principals, superintendents, curriculum directors, and supervisors.* Washington, DC: National Policy Board for Educational Administration.

Potter, L. (2001). Solving the principal shortage. *Principal, 80*(4), 34–37.

Richardson, L. (1999, June 23). Principal: A tougher job, fewer takers. *The Los Angeles Times,* p. A1.

Sergiovanni, T. J. (1992). *Moral leadership: Getting to the heart of school improvement*. San Francisco: Jossey-Bass.

Sergiovanni, T. J. (1996). *Leadership for the schoolhouse*. San Francisco: Jossey-Bass.

Sergiovanni, T. J. (2000). *The life world of leadership*. San Francisco: Jossey-Bass.

Shipman, N. J., Topps, B. W., & Murphy, J. (1998). *Linking the ISLLC standards to professional development and relicensure*. Paper presented to the annual conference of the American Educational Research Association, San Diego, CA.

Smith, M. L., Heinecke, W., & Noble, A. J. (1999). Assessment policy and political spectacle. *Teachers College Review, 101,* 157–191.

Study warns of shortage of qualified candidates for principalship. (1998, May). *Copy Editor, 55,* 1.

Thomson, S. (Ed.). (1993). *Principals of our changing schools: Knowledge and skill base*. Alexandria, VA: National Policy Board for Educational Administration.

U.S. Bureau of Labor Statistics. *Education Administrators*. 2000-01 Occupational Outlook Handbook. Retrieved November 26, 2001 from http://www.bls.gov/oco/

Van Meter, E., & Murphy, J. (1997). *Using ISLLC standards to strengthen preparation programs in school administration*. Washington, DC: Council of Chief State School Officers.

Wellstone, P. D. (2000). High stakes tests: A harsh agenda for America's children. *Education Review, 29,* 31–35.

Wilmore, E. (1999). Where there's a will there's a way: Creating university, public, private, and charter school collaboratives. *Education, 119*(3).

Wilmore, E. (2000). The changing role of school leadership preparation. *International Journal of Educational Reform, 9,* 349–359.

Wilmore, E. L. (2002). *Passing the principal ExCet exam: How to get certified the first time*. Thousand Oaks, CA: Corwin.

Wilmore, E., & McNeil, J. J., Jr. (1999). Who will lead our schools? *International Journal of Educational Reform, 8*(4).

Wilmore, E., & Thomas, C. (1998). Authentic administrative preparation: Linking theory to practice. *International Journal of Educational Reform, 7,* 172–177.

Worthen, B., Sanders, J., & Fitzpatrick, J. (1996). *Program evaluation, alternative approaches and practical guidelines* (2nd ed.). New York: Addison-Wesley.

Index

**CORWIN
PRESS**

The Corwin Press logo—a raven striding across an open book—
represents the happy union of courage and learning. We are a
professional-level publisher of books and journals for K-12 educators, and we are committed to creating and providing resources
that embody these qualities. Corwin's motto is "Success for
All Learners."